ADMINISTRATIVE LAW
AND PROCESS
IN A NUTSHELL

By

ERNEST GELLHORN

Professor of Law, University of Virginia

ST. PAUL, MINN.

WEST PUBLISHING CO.

1972

OUTLINE

OUTLINE

TABLE OF CASES

References are to Pages

TABLE OF CASES

X

TABLE OF CASES

TABLE OF CASES

TABLE OF CASES

TABLE OF CASES

TABLE OF CASES

TABLE OF CASES

TABLE OF CASES

†

ADMINISTRATIVE LAW
AND PROCESS

INTRODUCTION

As a rule, administrative agencies are created to deal with current crises, or with emerging problems, requiring supervision and flexible treatment. When Congress decided in the 19th century not to permit railroads to operate without close public control, it established the Interstate Commerce Commission—the first federal independent regulatory agency. As such, the ICC rules upon the rates a railroad may charge shippers, the routes which it serves, and (until 1970) the passenger service it provides. The phenomenal development of radio, with its attendant crowding of airwaves, brought about the creation of the Federal Radio Commission—the forerunner of today's Federal Communications Commission. This agency was charged with allocating licenses to stations to be operated "in the public interest." Following the stock market crash of 1929, the Securities and Exchange Commission was formed to assure the investor that the nation's money markets were financially sound. The SEC can prevent corporate securities from being issued or traded; its rules often set the limits on permissible conduct. More recently, when environmental pollution became a serious national concern, two administrative agencies—the Council on Environmental Quality and the Environmental Protection Agency—were established. And the clamor for effective consumer protection is bringing demands for increased power for the Federal Trade Commission and the creation of new agencies such as an independent Consumer Advocate or Department of Consumer Affairs.

While the major part of administrative law, and this text, concentrates on independent regulatory agencies such as the ICC, FTC, and SEC—since these bodies tend to present most of the questions of administrative law along with several unique ones—the administrative process is not limited to governmental departments separated from the legislative, executive or judicial branches. The rules of the administrative process invariably find application in the operation of executive departments (however, their application may differ), and, on occasion, even in legislative committees. Additional reasons for concentrating on federal administrative law are that state administrative agencies are generally governed by specific statutes which differ in each jurisdiction, and that the states eventually follow federal developments.

INTRODUCTION

There are today hundreds of administrative agencies performing innumerable tasks of government. Many were set up by the legislature to solve a crisis not amenable to simple legislative strictures. Often, as in the case of the SEC, their bright beginnings have been forerunners of a history of sound management and imaginative regulation. More often, however, bureaucratic lethargy and capture by the supposedly regulated industry followed the decline of public interest. So long as the public retains a keen interest in the agency's subject or activities—as exists today in the environment or consumer arenas—the pressure of publicity, news, and legislative scrutiny acts to assure vigorous and imaginative regulation. But when public interest wanes, the vitality of the agency declines proportionately. To be sure, there are exceptions. Public interest in the stock market has not continued at an extraordinary level since 1929. The strength of the SEC lies elsewhere: it would be contrary to the basic interest of the securities industry to capture the SEC; the money markets depend ultimately upon public confidence in the integrity of their operations and that confidence is dependent to a large degree on the appearance of the financial commuity's watchdog. In other words, agency structure is seldom the determining factor in its performance—except, perhaps, to hinder it.

Despite this essentially simple and obvious explanation, commentators and study groups continually look for magical solutions and propose radical surgery on the structure of most agencies as a panacea. Unfortunately, their critical recommendations are often based upon either an unhappy experience with one agency where their contentions are usually contradicted by those of other equally well-qualified observers in other agencies, or upon less obvious intuitive reactions unsupported by any empirical data. Again, their arguments are not the focal point of the administrative process or administrative law. This explanation of the administrative process, in other words, will concentrate on how it operates, on the "rules of the game"—not on how some would like to see it.

Despite this text's treatment of the administrative process as if it were a separate, somewhat self-contained body of law (such as Property or Contracts), it cannot be overemphasized that the reality of administrative practice is that administrative law as applied by the agencies and courts cannot be separated from the particular agency, its structure, personnel, legislative mission, and most importantly, its substantive law. This is borne out in this accurate summarization by Howard Westwood, a prominent Washington lawyer. "[A]dministrative agencies are very diverse. Each was created for a special set of problems. Each has a special legislative history behind its creation and each has, of necessity, developed its own mores without too close regard for the evolution of the mores of others."

CHAPTER I

JUDICIAL CONTROL: THE DELEGATION DOCTRINE

The study of administrative law can be viewed as an analysis of limits placed on the powers and actions of administrative agencies. These limits are imposed in many ways and at several points. One which we will examine at length is the procedures which courts, when reviewing agency orders, have demanded of agencies. Another is the rules specified by Congress in the Administrative Procedure Act ("APA"). Conceptually, however, the first question relates to the amount of legislative or judicial power which can be delegated initially to the agency by the legislature—the governmental body creating it. It is the question which first concerned the courts. (Interestingly, little attention has been paid to the delegation of executive power to an "independent" administrative agency.)

A. BASIC POLITICAL (CONSTITUTIONAL) THEORY

Our tripartite constitutional system of checks and balances roughly assigns law-making power to the legislature, law-enforcing power to the ex-

ecutive, and law-deciding power to the judiciary.
Administrative agencies do not fit neatly into any
one of these governmental groupings; their functions overlap into each. For example, the SEC
formulates law by writing rules which spell out
what disclosures must be made in a prospectus;
these rules may have the same effect as a law
passed by the legislature. The SEC then en-
forces these rules by prosecuting those who violate its regulations through disciplinary actions
against broker-dealers or through stop order proceedings against corporate issuers. Finally, the
SEC also acts as the judge and jury in deciding
whether its rules are violated by conducting adjudicatory hearings to determine guilt and to mete
out punishment. In other words, the SEC not
only writes the law but it also decides when and
whether the violators should be prosecuted, and
how they should be punished. In addition, administrative agencies are often unattached to
any of the three branches of government (executive, legislative or judiciary). Although the
commissioners—agency members—of the SEC
are presidential appointees (subject to Senate approval), the SEC is an independent agency; it is
not attached to the Congress nor is it a part of
any executive department.

The soundness of this combination of powers in
administrative agencies (in contrast to their func-

tional division by the Constitution) was once seriously questioned as being logically and legally in-
defensible. The attack assumed, erroneously, that
each governmental function is both readily distinguishable and mutually exclusive. Neither
premise is sound. Many, perhaps even most, traditional government bodies perform all three functions. For example, at the turn of the century
Congress passed the Sherman Antitrust Act prohibiting any "restraint on trade" tending to substantially reduce competition. This law was
passed by the legislature. However, the latter did
not decide whether an agreement by two steel
companies to fix the price at which they would sell
steel was an unlawful restraint. (The legislature
could have decided that question by specifying
that price-fixing is an unlawful restraint, but it
failed to do so.) The executive branch—acting
through the Justice Department—may decide this
"law-making" question by issuing rules against
price-fixing and by prosecuting the two steel companies in our example who elected not to observe
them (charging them with creating an unlawful
restraint on trade). If the steel companies then
decided to dispute the question, a court will "make
the law" (in the manner of a common law court)
except that its decision will be announced as in
favor of the government or of the steel companies.
The nub of the matter is that at each level—be it

the legislature, the executive or the judiciary—
the governmental body announces a "rule" which
involves law-making. Its rule governs past transactions making it, in effect, retroactive. In other
words, the executive and the judiciary constantly
engage in law-making; hence it is incorrect to assert that this function is in the exclusive domain
of the legislature.

The Federal Communication Commission's allocation of broadcast licenses illustrates law-making in the administrative context. Congress has
declared that radio and television station licenses
shall be awarded on the basis of "public interest,
convenience or necessity." Beyond this blandish-
ment the statute is devoid of criteria for determining what serves the "public interest," what
meets the standard of "convenience," or what constitutes "necessity." With only the statute to
guide them, broadcasters would have no guidelines
for evaluating how their performance would be
judged; applicants would be uncertain of the basis
upon which a station would be found to be best
able to serve the public interest. In giving meaning to this vague legislative mandate, the FCC relies upon its rulemaking (quasi-legislative) and
adjudicative (quasi-judicial) powers. Its "Blue
Book" rule, published in 1946, advises licensees
that they have a responsibility to offer "balanced"
programs—namely, that their programming mix

include entertainment, education, public issues, religion, "local live," and noncommercial ("sustaining") broadcasts. The FCC also imposes advertising limits. In issuing its rule the FCC acted as a legislature, spelling out in greater detail the meaning of "public interest," "convenience" and "necessity." Its action could also be viewed as execution of the law; on these criteria were based the issuance or revocation of a license, commonly an executive task. Furthermore, the FCC also has given greater meaning to these statutory terms through adjudicating (deciding) cases in the manner of a court.

The Commission was less certain, however, on standards for choosing between competing applicants for the same broadcast frequency; here it felt the need for additional facts and for a contested case. After a trial-type hearing it announced, in its decision for award of the license, "comparative hearing" standards which it would apply in deciding between applicants competing for the same license. These standards took account of the degree of local ownership of the applicant, whether his selection would increase media diversification in the community, which applicant had participated in civic affairs, and which was experienced in broadcasting (including the quality of his record).

The constitutional division of power, then, does not mean that only the legislature, in contrast to the executive or judiciary can "make the law." In the same vein, administrative agencies engage in law-making whenever they issue rules, enforce them, or adjudicate disputes. But this does not suggest that the principle of separation of powers is irrelevant and has no meaning in administrative, nee constitutional, law. Its great end is the dispersal of governmental authority to prevent absolutism. As Professor Jaffe observes, "Its object is the preservation of political safeguards against the capricious exercise of power; and, incidentally, it lays down the broad lines of efficient division of power." The legislature is the most "competent" law-making body of government and has basic responsibility for writing the law; the courts have similar responsibility for deciding controversies. However, the Constitution is not an organization chart. When the legislature determines that an administrative agency constitutes the best means of regulating an industry, it is not straight-jacketed by governmental theories current in 1789.

B. DEVELOPMENT OF DOCTRINE

The limitations on legislative delegation have not always been viewed as a balance between the authority needed for effective government regulation and the constraints required under a democratic, constitutional system. The judicial rhetoric of the delegation doctrine (or as it is sometimes called, the nondelegation doctrine) is fond of absolutes. Typical is the Supreme Court's early categorical imperative pronounced in Field v. Clark, 143 U.S. 649, 692, 12 S.Ct. 495, 504 (1892): "That Congress cannot delegate legislative power . . . is a principle universally recognized as vital to the integrity and maintenance of the system of government ordained by the Constitution." This oft-repeated statement suggests that only the narrowest delegation of law-making power, if any, will be upheld. That the opposite has occurred, of course, is history. The story of the decline, rise, and fall of the delegation doctrine is foundational to an understanding of the administrative process as it operates today. It tells us not only what the boundaries of permissible delegation are, but also about one technique for limiting arbitrary administrative action.

Despite strident condemnations of any congressional delegation of its law-making functions, the Supreme Court has sustained one delegation after another. In withstanding these challenges, the doctrine has undergone change. In the 19th century, the Supreme Court approved the delegation of authority to the President to act when a *named contingency* occurred. That is, the President was properly authorized to lift trade embargoes when the United States' neutrality in commerce was again observed by France and England (The Brig Aurora, 11 U.S. (7 Cranch) 382 (1813)), or to levy retaliatory tariffs when foreign nations raised their duties on American agricultural products (Field v. Clark, supra). Perhaps the most striking feature is that only two cases reached the Supreme Court in the nation's first century, in which each challenge involved congressional authorization of specific Presidential action upon his determination that a narrowly defined contingency had occurred. While only the President could lift the embargo or impose a higher tariff, he was obliged to act when the contingency occurred, *and* the level of the duty was established by Congress. On the other hand, the existence of the contingency was not the simple fact question that the Court assumed.

As government undertook more complex tasks and congressional delegations became more expansive, the challenges increased and the inadequacy of the named contingency formula became apparent—but the delegations continued to be upheld. By now they obviously involved more than "executive" authority to determine whether a particular event had occurred. The doctrinal formulation responded to this change. Three cases, illustrating this development, required the Court to decide whether Congress could delegate the following authority: to the Secretary of the Treasury to set a minimum quality standard for imported tea; * to the Secretary of Agriculture to "make such rules and regulations" (punishable by criminal penalties) as would insure that public lands were protected from fire and destruction; and to the President to investigate the "differences in costs of production of articles" between the United States and other countries in order to adjust tariff rates up to 50 percent to "equalize" these costs. In upholding each delegation, the Court developed several verbal formulations— that Congress had established a "primary standard" for the tea tasters, that the Secretary of Agriculture was only exercising a "power to fill up the details" in regulating use of public lands, and that the President's flexible tariff authority was guided by an "intelligible principle." In candid asides in each decision, the Court conceded that it was influenced by the fact that "Congress [had] legislated on the subject as far as was reasonably practicable." It recognized "that it is difficult to define the line which separates legis-

* For those who might question the significance of these cases today, see the recent attempt—and failure—of President Nixon to abolish the tea-tasting board as an unnecessary governmental function. New York Times, May 13, 1970, at 16, col. 4.

lative power to make laws, from administrative authority to make regulations."

In each case the Court paid obeisance to the so-called named contingency theory and then went on to redefine the nondelegation doctrine. The doctrinal formulations of a "primary standard," of "power to fill up the details," or of an "intelligible principle," however, only obscured the fact that law-making power was now lodged in non-legislative hands. The reason is obvious. The practical necessities of modern government demanded delegation of law-making authority. The doctrine of separation of powers could not become the altar upon which governmental operations meeting the country's felt needs could be sacrificed. The constitutional provision that "All legislative power herein granted shall be vested in a Congress of the United States" (Article I, § 1), is counterbalanced by the equally authoritative power granted Congress "To make all laws which shall be necessary and proper" (Article I, § 8). The policy justifications for creating administrative agencies—the need for continuous expert supervision, specialization, and systematic and uniform regulation, as well as competing demands on limited legislative time, to name but a few—forced the decline of the delegation doctrine, oddly enough, before it had ever been applied to overturn a single congressional delegation.

Doctrinally, however, the delegation doctrine was not dead. Instead the Court had shifted its ground from its original purpose of preventing the delegation of law-making power to the objective of requiring every delegation to be accompanied by a meaningful standard. When it approved broad phrases such as "just and reasonable rates" for application to railroad regulation, "public interest, convenience, or necessity" for guidance in the issuance of radio broadcast licenses, and "unfair methods of competition" for governance of competitive business conduct, many observers wondered whether the doctrine had become nothing more than mere verbiage. Could any congressional delegation be found wanting in an "intelligible principle"? The cases in the Depression years invalidating the National Industrial Recovery Act were an explicit answer; the doctrine was alive and well, if only for a brief period.

The NIRA was one of Congress' responses to the economic crisis of the 1930s. Among other things, it authorized the President to prohibit interstate shipment of contraband oil (that is, oil produced illegally in a state). When this provision of the Act was challenged, the Court, for the first time in its history, declared a congressional delegation void. Panama Refining Co. v. Ryan, 293 U.S. 388, 55 S.Ct. 241 (1935). The ostensible ground for the decision, in what came to be known as the "Hot Oil" case, was the failure of Congress to constrict the President's authority within definable limits. (The Act did not spell out when he was to act; in fact the standards in the Act were held to be self-contradictory.) When compared with previously approved congressional delegations, the Court's decision cannot be reconciled or rationalized—certainly not by Congress' subsequently successful amendment which limited Presidential discretion to act when supply and demand became so imbalanced as to "unduly burden or restrict" interstate commerce. The defect was extraneous. In administering the NIRA, the National Recovery Administration—the agency assigned the job of performing this task of the President—failed to observe minimum procedural decencies. Not only was the criminally enforceable petroleum code unpublished and unavailable to affected parties, but also a careful examination disclosed that the code had in fact been amended out of existence. Jaffe's description captures the atmosphere:

> The President immediately supplied the missing provisions, thus making true the state of facts which had been assumed by all persons and courts to have existed. Nevertheless, the Supreme Court refused to treat the Code as properly before it. Those who heard and

participated in the argument were struck by the almost gleeful eagerness with which the Court probed into the unsavory story (though it had previously been completely advised). (Jaffe, Judicial Control of Administrative Action 62 (1965).)

The *Hot Oil* decision, then, is sui generis, and its only and valuable consequence was to speed the creation of a system for publishing administrative rules and regulations in what is now the Federal Register and the Code of Federal Regulations.

Five months later, in the "Sick Chicken" case, the Court invalidated a criminal prosecution for violation of the Live Poultry Code issued under another section of the NIRA. Schechter Poultry Corp. v. United States, 295 U.S. 495, 55 S.Ct. 837 (1935). The delegation here seemingly had no limit. The President was "to formulate codes of fair competition" for any industry if the code "will tend to effectuate the policy of this title." (Yet in the *Hot Oil* case the Court could not discern a consistent policy in the Act.) Moreover, the codes were comprehensive, including elaborate regulation of prices, minimum wages and maximum hours. The Court's concern, again, was not limited to—or, perhaps, not directed primarily at—the undefined nature of the delegation since it had approved almost equally broad

[*18*]

grants of law-making power to the ICC and FTC. Once again the Court disdained the lack of procedural protections afforded those likely to be affected by the codes, namely, the lack of notice, the lack of an opportunity to be heard, and the lack of judicial review. It carefully distinguished acceptable delegations of similarly broad powers to the ICC, the FTC and the Federal Radio Commission (the FCC's predecessor) by pointing to their procedural safeguards. The Court apparently sensed that dominant industrial groups in fact held power and used it in their own favor when drafting industry codes.

Even though Congress has delegated constantly increasing law-making power to governmental officials since 1935, the Supreme Court has not invalidated any federal statute delegating law-making powers to government officials on delegation grounds in the intervening years. The authority to determine "excessive profits," to "liquidate" savings and loan associations, to fix "maximum prices and wages," and to "allocate" vast quantities of water among water-short states are among the many delegations which have been upheld.

Obviously the question must again be asked, does the doctrine have any vitality? One answer is that the Court has never disavowed it, nor has it suggested that there are no limits on the power of Congress to delegate its authority. No subsequent federal enactment has had the "imposing generality" of the NIRA without including important procedural protections against arbitrary administrative actions. Subsequent decisions, in other words, can be distinguished by careful analysis.

The closest recent brush with an invalid delegation was actually invited by the government in Kent v. Dulles, 357 U.S. 116, 78 S.Ct. 1113 (1958). In order to avoid difficult constitutional questions on travel restrictions, the Court, however, rejected the Secretary of State's argument that his power to issue passports was wholly discretionary. Instead the Court read the statute narrowly by finding an acceptable standard in the purpose of the enactment and in the prior administrative practice in which it was applied. That is, the Court narrowed the delegation to an acceptable level and then approved it. It is also noteworthy that a personal freedom—the right to travel—not private economic interests, was at stake. On the other hand, it is true that exceedingly broad delegations are universally upheld by federal courts. E. g., Permian Basin Area Rate Cases, 390 U.S. 747, 83 S.Ct. 1344 (1968); Arizona v. California, 373 U.S. 546, 83 S.Ct. 1468 (1963); Amalgamated Meat Cutters v. Connally, 333 F.Supp. 737 (D.D.C. 1971); California Teachers Ass'n v. Newport Mesa Unified School Dist., 333 F.Supp. 436 (C.D.Cal.1971). The dramatic *Hot Oil* and *Sick Chicken* cases have had little impact on legislative practices or judicial decisions in terms of requiring precise standards or of limiting administrative authority. Thus, to the extent that the delegation doctrine is designed to restrict grants of law-making powers to administrative agencies within discernible standards, it is interesting but not very potent history.

Despite the fact that the Federal constitutional theory of separation of powers does not apply to the states, their courts are more restrictive and have frequently disapproved the delegation of law-making powers to state agencies if the enabling legislation lacks "standards." At times state courts have relied upon state constitutional (separation of power) grounds. Judicial disapproval in the states occurs most frequently where the delegated power involves the regulation of a profession (from plumbers to doctors) or the private use of real property (specifically, zoning). State court opinions repeat the shopworn phrases of "no reasonable standard," even though the courts' concern is obviously premised upon the fact that these delegations frequently are made to petty officials, involve an individual's livelihood, and appear susceptible to discrim-

inatory administration. In any case, the pattern
among the states is uneven.

C. ANOTHER CONSTITUTIONAL DIMENSION

The delegation doctrine has another dimension
—one which is frequently overlooked. The due
process clause of the Constitution has been applied to limit delegation of power to administrative agencies. In this context, due process means
that a person may not be deprived of life, liberty
or property by an administrative agency without
a reasonable opportunity, appropriate under the
circumstances, to challenge the agency's action,
or without a fair warning of the limits of permissible conduct. Thus, it is improper to authorize an agency to set railroad rates without allowing the regulated railroad an opportunity to show
the agency or a court that the rate is not "just
and reasonable"; the potential that a discriminatory rate will result is too great. Nor can agencies be delegated adjudicatory power to determine criminal guilt or to impose criminal penalties, although power to impose a civil fine or issue a remedial order is appropriate. The constitutional guaranty of a jury trial, and other
procedural protections governing the trial of
criminal prosecutions, restrict the administrative
domain.

It may also be a violation of due process to delegate law-making power to private groups disguised as an administrative agency. For example, a majority of coal producers cannot set industry prices and wages, even if Congress seeks to delegate them the power, since the majority will must be exercised through a governmental body. See Carter v. Carter Coal Co., 298 U.S. 238, 56 S.Ct. 855 (1936). While state licensing boards are frequently (probably usually) constituted by those already members of the profession, power cannot be delegated to a private trade group to appoint a majority of the licensing board which issues and revokes licenses. The reasoning behind this rule is that the minority or outsider may not be treated fairly, that self-interest should not be institutionalized in this manner. On the other hand, limited resources and the need for expertise often dictate the inclusion of private parties as members of public agencies.

Courts have also invalidated delegations of adjudicative power on the grounds of "void for vagueness"—a doctrine subsumed under the due process clause—where the standard for illegal action is defined broadly and the sanctions are severe. Again the licensing cases are illustrative. A dentist or mortician cannot be denied renewal of his license for "unfair advertising" where no advance warnings are given concerning the limits of acceptable conduct. Note that this "void for vagueness" doctrine in administrative (as contrasted to constitutional) law does not apply to delegations of law-making power, since the agency's action must precede any impact of the challenged rule. On the other hand, no contravention of either the due process or the judicial power (Art. III, § 2) clauses results from conferring adjudicative power on an administrative agency, such as a workman's compensation board, to decide whether an employer is liable to his employee for injuries incurred in the employer's business. Crowell v. Benson, 285 U.S. 22, 52 S.Ct. 285 (1932). The Court emphasized that judicial review was preserved under the delegated plan.

While it must be conceded that all cases simply will not parse, nonetheless the due process branch of the delegation doctrine has continuing vitality, particularly in judging the validity of law-deciding (adjudicative) power. Its application involves a balance among the need for regulation, the ability to provide the regulation in some other way (or in such a manner as to avoid potentially discriminatory or unfair results on the regulated group), and the severity of the sanction applied when the legislative or administrative mandate is not observed.

D. DELEGATION—TODAY AND TOMORROW

The delegation doctrine raises peculiarly sensitive issues. Its practical and constitutional problems are co-extensive with Marbury v. Madison, 5 U.S. (1 Cranch) 137 (1803) where, you recall, the Supreme Court asserted its power to determine the constitutionality of laws enacted by the Congress and President. Specifically, when the nondelegation doctrine is applied, one branch of the government (the judiciary) overrules the choice of another (the legislature—and, when the President has concurred, also the executive). Other restraints on administrative action are either cooperative efforts of the two branches (e. g., Congress defines the agency's authority and the courts confine the agency to its conferred power) or the unilateral actions of one (e. g., legislative oversight and funding; executive appointment). Perhaps this is the reason for the inconsistent, stormy history and somewhat confused status of the doctrine.

Originally conceived as a limitation on the authority of the Congress to delegate legislative, executive, or judicial *functions* to administrative agencies, the nondelegation doctrine claims few, if any, adherents. Nor has it ever been applied at the federal level to prevent reasonably circumscribed delegations of law-making, law-enforcing, or law-deciding power to agencies or administrators. However, it does express a legitimate concern that when delegating *power* to an agency or administrator, the legislature should, indeed must, impose some restraints.

The "standards" technique of requiring that Congress spell out meaningful standards to guide administrators in fulfilling their assigned tasks, to advise courts in judging whether the administrators' actions are authorized, and to inform regulated persons what rules must be obeyed, has proven unsound and unworkable. Agencies are frequently established to develop and implement solutions or to regulate current activities; the legislature can neither foresee what actions the agency should take nor constantly revise the mandate as conditions change. To force Congress to act otherwise is to ask it to perform an impossible task and, therefore, to invite chaos. This is not to say, however, that Congress should not (or that it does not) spell out an agency's mandate as carefully as possible. The delegation doctrine does not address itself to what Congress should do, but rather to what it *must* do. And today it seems clear that Congress constitutionally is not required to do very much affirmatively. It is not required to spell out standards as clearly as it can, to revise standards as policy develops, or to provide guidelines for judging agency authority. Bowing to the needs of a complex society, the Supreme Court apparently has concluded that Congress is free to identify the problem—such as protecting consumers from "unfair competition," or the public from "environmental hazards"—and then to tell the agency merely, "go solve it."

The demise of the "standards" test, however, has not meant that there are no negative restraints on Congressional delegations. Agencies may not now be delegated uncontrolled discretion or granted unlimited power. What has happened is that the delegation doctrine is now cloaked in the language of due process and measured by the procedural safeguards surrounding the agency's exercise of power. Agency performance rather than the legislative delegation is becoming the critical standard. Cf. Kent v. Dulles, 357 U.S. 116, 78 S.Ct. 1113 (1958). The base point, or ultimate protection, depending on one's point of view, of this approach is the usual requirement that before a person is adversely (and finally) affected by administrative action or sanction he must be assured an opportunity for judicial review. At one time this meant that delegations of law-making power to administrative agencies were disturbed because judicial review was not authorized; today delegations are saved by broadly construing review statutes, by widening standards for "standing" to seek review or by extending common law remedies. Where procedural safeguards of notice, of a right to be heard and of a right to confront adverse evidence are not available—particularly when individual rights of liberty and dignity are at stake—the delegated authority may be overturned on a due process ground. It has been urged, however, that instead of overturning the delegation of legislative power, the court should require administrators "as rapidly as feasible" to supply meaningful standards and to structure administrative discretion substantively and procedurally. In this context discretion includes not only the agency's enforcement of a rule (such as the FCC's balanced program regulation) but also its selective non-enforcement of the rule (such as the granting of a license to an FCC applicant who does not meet the "Bluebook" standard). If this view is adopted, attention will focus on what the agency has done to enunciate standards and to provide fair procedures where the legislature was not supplied specific directions.

CHAPTER II

on Admin. agencies

NONJUDICIAL CONTROLS: THE POLITICAL PROCESS

Any discussion of the functions and powers of administrative agencies is incomplete, especially when the agencies operate within a constitutional democracy, unless it also considers the controls imposed from nonjudicial sources. Agency authority does not always mean that an agency can act even if it has the will to do so. For example, the statutory authority of the Justice Department and the Federal Trade Commission probably gives them power to seek dismemberment of the automobile manufacturing companies under the antitrust laws in order to increase the likelihood of competition in the country's largest industry. Government lawyers, economists, agency personnel, and outside critics frequently call for this action. It is anomalous, at best, to attack combinations of chrysanthemum growers, janitorial service companies, sellers of kitchenware and manufacturers of bed springs, each having comparatively minimal economic impact, while at the same time oligopolistic concentrations in major industries are ignored. Past and current inhibition on agency action against the auto behemoths lies not in the agencies' power but elsewhere. This chapter explores these controls.

A. LEGISLATIVE CONTROL

In one sense, the delegation doctrine is an expression of legislative control of agency action. The legislature creates the agency and the organic act sets the limit of the agency's power, directs the manner of its operation, and determines the focus of its attention. The delegation doctrine, then, is a judicial attempt, in broad outline only, to require the legislature to exercise this control. As a practical matter, however, such legislative control is meaningless. More meaningful, perhaps, but still limited is the judicial implementation of legislative control, in the course of reviewing an agency's actions, by determining whether the agency has acted ultra vires or has complied with the legislative mandate.

Other legislative controls have greater impact on agency operations. One control, of course, is by additional legislation. If the legislature is dissatisfied with an agency's course, it can simply change the agency's mandate or reverse its decision. For example, in 1964 the Congress concluded that the FTC's proposed warning label on cigarette products and advertising was too harsh and substituted its own rule; it repeated this tactic in 1970 when the FCC and FTC indicated that they would place further restrictions on cigarette promotions. Alternatively, legislation is used to increase agency authority, such as recent mandates to the FDA to regulate hazardous household substances and dangerous toys. When Congress was concerned about the fairness of agency procedures, it set minimum procedural standards by adopting the APA. And in order to assure that agencies assess the environmental impact of their decision, it now requires (by section 102 of the Environmental Protection Act, 42 U.S.C.A. § 4332) that agency decisions include consideration of the environmental impact and specify how environmental needs are being served. See, e. g., Calvert Cliffs' Coordinating Comm., Inc. v. AEC, 449 F.2d 1109 (D.C. Cir. 1971).

Other legislative controls are equally diverse and effective in checking, but not always in assuring, proper administrative action. Agency performance and decision making is affected by legislative appropriations (the power of the purse), investigations (to acquire information, to expose misdeeds), the continuing supervision of standing or special committees, and the operation of the appointment process (senatorial courtesy, the power of approval). The legislature often plays an "ombudsman" role by interceding with the agency—even on particular cases—on behalf of interested clients.

Notice, these pressures are all political rather than legal in that the legislature does not rely on legal sanctions to make its point. Nevertheless, its wishes are always heard and usually obeyed. To the extent that these pressures reflect a legislative consensus they are not troublesome in a democratic system. However, they frequently reflect the wishes of powerful individuals (committee chairmen) unchecked by the legislative process.*

B.   EXECUTIVE CONTROL

When an administrative agency operates within an executive department, the President exercises direct and total control. His power, in the first instance, is the simple and ultimate sanction of appointment and removal. To be sure, there have been isolated examples where the administrator's political importance forced the President, as a practical matter, not to exercise this power. But their infrequency attests to the extent of presidential control; the power of senatorial concurrence has not been a significant restraint.

Agencies outside the executive departments—such as the SEC—are similarly subject to execu-

* Administrative action "improperly influenced" by congressional pressure may be reversed on review, however. See D. C. Fed'n of Civic Ass'ns v. Volpe, 3 E.R.C. 1143 (D.C. Cir. Oct. 12, 1971), cert. denied, 92 S.Ct. 1290 (1972) (Three Sisters Bridge); pp. 232 infra.

tive control. Several differences exist, however. These commissioners are appointed for a term of years, five to be exact, and their terms do not coincide with the President's. While this difference can be significant at the beginning of a President's term in office, it does not mean that the President is powerless. He has the power to appoint (or demote) the agency chairman. Since the members' terms are staggered and agencies are often required to be politically balanced (for example, no more than three of the five members of the SEC may be members of one political party), the President invariably can make critical appointments early in his term and thereby control the agency's policy direction. Presidents Eisenhower, Kennedy, and Nixon each radically altered the direction of the NLRB (where political balance is not required) within almost a year of assuming office.

There are, in addition, other restraints or pressures that a President can apply to recalcitrant agencies. The most dramatic is the removal of an incumbent commissioner. Practically, it is not used because of the political risks and, even more importantly, because of questions concerning the President's authority. The latter is not without significance. One early case, involving a postmaster, suggested that the President had sweeping powers of removal, and that Congress could not limit his authority without violating the Constitution (Article II). Myers v. United States, 272 U.S. 52, 47 S.Ct. 21 (1926). Postmasters, however, do not generally make significant policy decisions nor engage in quasi-judicial functions. Moreover, at the time in question, postmasters were appointed by the President (subject to the Senate's consent) for four years unless "sooner suspended or removed."

When President Roosevelt relied upon *Myers* a decade later to discharge an unsympathetic chairman of the FTC, the Supreme Court refused to disregard the statutory limitation on the President's removal power. With respect to the FTC, the President's statutory authority for removal was limited to "inefficiency, neglect of duty, or malfeasance in office"—and none of these charges had been leveled against the chairman. In Humphrey's Executor v. United States, 295 U.S. 602, 55 S.Ct. 869 (1935), the Court suggested that these statutory limitations were necessary to maintain the constitutional, tripartite division of power. But the Court's reasoning is questionable. Insofar as the agency exercises quasi-judicial power, it seems apparent that Congress may legitimately decide—or even be constitutionally required as an element of due process— to hedge against executive domination. This need and constitutional base evaporates when an agency's task is to carry out the legislative mandate—that is, when the agency performs only executive tasks.

Later decisions have not further defined the limits of executive control. Perhaps the only current significance these cases hold for us today is that in several agencies (the FCC, FPC, and SEC) the members are not statutorily protected against summary removal from office. (These agencies were created after *Myers* indicated that no limitation on the President's removal power was valid and before *Humphrey's* rule that Congress could and, perhaps, must limit his authority.) Nevertheless, President Nixon apparently did not wish to test the limits of his removal authority when one FTC member recently passed the compulsory retirement age; instead the President finessed the issue by exempting (under statutory authority) the commissioner from retirement provisions until early 1973.*

Presidential power over administrative regulation also has a broader base. He controls agency actions in many ways. Like the Congress, the President relies initially upon his control of agency appropriations. Agency budgets are reviewed

---

* Technically the removal power could still be tested by the FTC Commissioner since the exemption did not extend to the end of the latter's term. See 35 Fed.Reg. 17,-703 (Nov. 18, 1970) (Executive Order 11568); 37 Fed.Reg. 2,565 (February 3, 1972) (Executive Order 11642).

and revised by the Office of Management and Budget before they are submitted to the Congress; OMB is the President's management arm. Presidential controls extend beyond budgetary allowances, however. With the assistance of OMB, the President regulates the agency's legislative proposals in that his disapproval generally blocks the agency from the Congress and OMB's approval is the sine qua non of passage in most instances. New legislative mandates (and appropriations) approved by the Congress must win the President's approval. OMB also is active in approving the creation and staffing of supergrades—although the latter is a political reality rather than a legal requirement. Agency organization may be drastically altered by the President under the reorganization acts (here the Congress has the veto). And, as was noted in discussing the early development of the delegation doctrine, in some cases the President may in fact participate in administrative decisions. For instance, tariff levels and foreign airline route allocations are subject to Presidential approval. Cumulatively these powers of control over agency action seem significant. In individual agencies and cases, they frequently are quite limited.

C. INDIRECT POLITICAL CONTROL

Although not required to submit their record to the voters periodically, administrative authorities, like courts, are aware of election returns. This is not to say that agencies trim their sails merely to curry executive or legislative favor— or to avoid their displeasure. In fact, agencies are so removed from the voter's perception of central political issues that the more frequent complaint is that Congress and the President treat the agencies like unwanted step-children, starving them of attention and support until they get into serious trouble and reflect adversely on their guardians. More effective in controlling agency action is the glare of public exposure— usually to point out misdeeds, but also to goad the agency into action.

Thus in recent times both the FDA and FTC have been publicly castigated by private study groups for failing to fulfill their legislative mandates to protect consumers from dangerous drugs and deceptive advertising. In the past, particularly during the late forties and the fifties, such public criticism was aimed primarily at acts of favoritism by, and the corruption of, an occasional agency official. The current crises in energy supplies (brown-outs), telecommunications systems (jammed telephone circuits), and mass transit designs (choked freeways and bankrupt railroads), will undoubtedly once again focus public attention on the major regulatory agencies. The recent conclusions of the Ash Council (President Nixon's commission to study and recommend government reorganization) that these failures stem from agency structure which in turn could be corrected by reliance on single administrators rather than multi-member commissions, by limiting the administrator's adjudicative responsibilities, and by appointment of a special administrative court of review, is only the first of what promise to be many responses.

While this "publicity control" may result from reports commissioned by the Congress or the President, the most frequent public critiques today—and probably the most effective—are the exposés emanating from investigative journalism (by radio, tv, magazines) or private study groups now symbolized by Ralph Nader's "Raiders." Only occasionally have internal self-studies by the agency (such as the "Pentagon Papers" inquiring into the escalation of the Vietnam War) served this function; their release is usually at the agency's discretion and, while confession may be good for the soul, agencies instinctively recognize that adverse publicity may hamper future activity. On the other hand, public reports on agency performance are not the preserve of any pact.

In several countries and a few jurisdictions in the United States, extra-legal controls on agency performance are institutionalized in a public "ombudsman"—a public official, usually responsible to the legislature, with broad authority to investigate individual complaints of administrative misconduct, to report on them, and to make recommendations. As the federal government continues to increase in size it seems likely that such public intermediaries to whom private citizens may submit their grievances, will proliferate. The Administrative Conference—an administrative agency having the task of studying and recommending better procedures to other agencies (that is, an administrative agency whose function is to study other agencies)—is the closest institutional counterpart. However, its mandate does not include matters of substantive policy or individual complaints, except where individual injustices stimulate investigation into general procedural problems. On the other hand, Congress' jealousy of its legislative prerogatives and a legitimate concern that the ombudsman will quickly become merely another bureaucratic layer insulating governmental authorities from the citizenry, suggests that the private critic will play a significant role in the future. Recent developments permitting freer access by citizens to agency files and agency decision making (through expansion of the concept of "standing" to appeal or intervene) further suggest an expanded role for private, nongovernmental critics in restraining agency actions.

Public disclosure as a control on administrative authority is supported by long, democratic tradition and the theory of open government. Muckraking is a journalistic tradition which relies, in part, upon access to information about governmental operations. The recent amendment of section 3 of the APA, by the so-called Freedom of Information Act (5 U.S.C.A. § 552), sought to strengthen and codify the "people's right to know." It does not clearly answer the question, however, "to know *what*?" Section 3 compels every federal agency to make "promptly available to *any* person" records in the agency's files which are not otherwise exempt from disclosure. The exemptions were designed to protect documents classified for national security, internal management and privacy reasons. As yet it is too early to assess the actual impact of section 3. The burden of denying access has now been switched to the agency; the requesting party may now sue wherever he resides as well as where the records are located; the statutory presumption favors disclosure. As a practical matter, however, copying and location fees, strict in-

terpretations of the identified records requirement, broad readings of the nine statutory exemptions, and the cost of bringing suit, all restrict citizen access. Although the strongest support for amending section 3 came from newsmen,
none of the media have brought an action under
the Act during its first two years of existence.
One can only speculate whether this means that
reporters are reluctant to press their rights or
that agencies have correctly read the statutory
handwriting and granted newsman access. (Incidentally, section 3 of the APA has relevance
to discovery of information from agency files, so
we will consider it again.)

Despite the impact which publicity can have on
administrative agencies, it should be noted that,
unlike most other controls, the "publicity control" tends to be a relatively crude weapon. A
non-expert public is likely to condemn an entire
agency for one official's misconduct or for the
agency's failure in a single, highly visible program. Moreover, to be effective, criticism of
agency performance frequently depends on continuing scrutiny, and the span of the public's attention is very brief. Nonetheless, the possibility and fact of public exposure operates as a significant yet unmeasurable restraint on administrative action. It is a gross control, smoothing
out the worst points of friction in the administrative process.

CHAPTER III

AN OVERVIEW OF JUDICIAL REVIEW

Closely related to—and indeed, often inseparable from—the many controls which limit agency options, is the process of court review of agency action (or inaction). This judicial review scrutinizes the fairness of agency procedures and the authority for an agency's substantive decisions. The availability and scope of review has a direct bearing not only upon the matter under review, but also upon agency procedures and substantive policies.

Consequently, a basic understanding of the review process is necessary for comprehension of agency acquisition of information and its decision making process. For example, the procedural elements of most adjudicative hearings—insuring that the affected party be given notice, the opportunity to be heard, and the occasion to test unfavorable evidence—stem from constitutional standards pressed upon agencies during judicial review of their final administrative orders. Also, the narrowness of judicial review, the frequency and length of agency hearings, and the inconvenience and cost of providing a complete transcript, result in the requirement that findings accompany final agency action to facilitate judicial review. Nevertheless, this text postpones an extended analysis of the various avenues for obtaining judicial relief and the administrative law doctrines applicable to court review until the administrative decision making process has been explored. There is no magic in this sequence. It proceeds on the assumption—largely untested—that unless one understands what the agency has done and why, the review process will remain unduly mysterious.

Administrative action may take many forms. An order may grant a tv station license, deny a workmen's compensation claim, prohibit an unfair trade practice, make possible the collection of wage reparations by an illegally discharged employee, levy a tax, or award a second class mailing bounty. Also the administrative order may be interim or final. Again, the directly affected person may have been named as a party and may have participated in a hearing almost indistinguishable from the trial of a civil suit; or he may have participated only on his own initiative (and even then have been given merely an opportunity to submit his views in writing). However, regardless of the form of the order or the procedure relied upon, a significant administrative sanction generally cannot be imposed without an opportunity for judicial review. There are, of course, exceptions. Review may not be available until after a tax or fine has been paid or an interim license suspended. The discretionary decision of whether to prosecute, which is usually not reviewable, may work a hardship equal to any other. The thrust of current developments, however, is to narrow the exceptions, to open up additional avenues for judicial review, and to require that judicial consideration precede administrative execution.

The function of judicial review is to assure that the administrator's action is (a) authorized—i. e., within his delegated authority—and not ultra vires, and (b) not an abuse of discretion—i. e., that it represent a reasonable choice supported by the available evidence. It assures that, when challenged, the administrative action evidences that it has not encroached excessively on private rights. Review is generally provided for by statute or by common law precedents. If the administrative sanction involves a significant personal or property interest, the right of review may also have a constitutional (due process) foundation. While the administrator may, in a particular case, exercise self-restraint (and thus stay within proper bounds), courts traditionally have been the ultimate protectors of individual rights against the misuse of executive power.

Judicial review legitimates the application of administrative sanctions. It is a procedure for public accountability of the administrative process (and, in this connection, is an extension of the "publicity control"). Furthermore, it is important in assuring the acceptability—particularly to the subjects—of the administrative process. Judicial review acts as a corollary restraint to the broad powers frequently (and, under current interpretations of the delegation doctrine, properly) vested in administrative authorities.

In the process of legitimating administrative action, judicial review operates primarily as a check upon the administrative branch of the government. There is, however, a second aspect of judicial review which is receiving increased attention—namely, such a review may force the administrator to discharge his statutory obligations. For example, at the urgings of private groups not parties to the original proceedings, courts have directed the AEC to consider the environmental impact of an atomic power plant before permitting its construction, and have ordered the EPA to hear a petition that pesticide regulations be rewritten—even though the private parties seeking the license or immediately affected by the regulations did not complain. Favoritism of private interests by an administrator may be as prejudicial as unwarranted encroachment.

On the other hand, the function of judicial review is not to insure the correctness of the administrative decision. That is a matter of judgment which Congress has delegated to the administrator and not to the reviewing court. Rather, judicial review tests whether the agency (a) has exceeded its constitutional or statutory authority, (b) has properly interpreted the applicable law, (c) has conducted a fair proceeding, and (d) has not acted capriciously or unreasonably.

Despite the seemingly broad sweep of this judicial inquiry, most agency decisions are left untouched. This is undoubtedly due in part to the fact that an administrator who knows that his actions can be reviewed and, if arbitrary, overturned will take pains to see that his conduct can withstand close examination. A more important feature, however, is that the scope of review is hedged by many restrictions. Courts reviewing administrative decisions—like appellate courts scrutinizing trial court or jury actions—defer to the agency's judgment if it has some rational basis. The agency's specialized expertise, coupled with its broad legislative mandate (which is not given to the court), is usually controlling. The standard of judicial review varies with the significance of the issue to the rights of the appealing party and with the competence of the court (versus the agency) to decide the issue. Generally, a review court will interpret questions of agency authority independently from the administrator's recommendations. (The cases, however, are replete with exceptions.) These statutory interpretations cover both substantive and adjective law.

For example, the scope of the Federal Trade Commission's jurisdiction over business practices "in commerce" is ultimately a court decision. Similarly, it is for the court, rather than the agency, to determine not only whether a public housing authority in terminating a tenant's lease is required to give the tenant notice and afford him a hearing to test the validity of the housing authority's action, but also, if required, to state what kind of notice and hearing are minimally adequate. These issues are generally viewed as questions of law which are subject to unlimited judicial review.

Courts frequently maintain that questions of law are sharply differentiated from questions of fact on judicial review. Law questions are theoretically subject to full review; that is, the court will determine the correctness of the interpretation and will freely substitute its judgment for the agency's on law issues. Fact questions, on the contrary, are reviewed by the court only to the extent of ascertaining whether the administrative finding is supported by substantial evidence when the whole record is considered. Inferences are reversible only if unreasonable or without a rational basis; the court need not agree with the administrator's conclusion so long as a reasonable administrator could have reached the challenged result.

This law-fact-inference distinction is easier to state than to apply; it has bedeviled the courts. Judicial applications reveal a post hoc justification rather than the development of criteria useful in distinguishing one from the other. The standard of review is not objective. The courts have a wide choice between intervening in agency determinations on the one hand and exercising restraint on the other. It is neither surprising nor infrequent, then, that what is viewed by one judge as a fact question requiring deference represents a question of law calling for de novo judicial reconsideration by another. Even then, however, it is not unusual for a court to defer to the agency's conclusion, but on different grounds. Here the judge viewing the issue as a question of law may accept the administrator's statutory interpretation as plausible and therefore not to be disturbed, especially if the administrator has special competence in the area and the interpretation will significantly affect his ability to fulfill the legislative objective.

As this brief discussion suggests, the law of judicial review does not lend itself to easy generalization. There are many limitations to judicial review. It is designed only to establish minimum standards. Courts do not require that agencies adopt the fairest or the most efficient procedures. Judicial review only checks agency abuses; courts do not supervise agency actions. Review does not assure a "correct" result; the court's role rather is confined to determining whether the administrator has acted within his delegated discretion. And, of course, the possibility of review has at most but a limited impact where review is not sought—the practical result in most cases. Other factors may restrict the impact of judicial review. For example, the option of review may come too late to be useful to the aggrieved party. Or even when review is sought, the agency may avoid reversal by altering the procedure or justification (on remand) without any change in the substantive result.

Yet despite the "limited office" of judicial review, it is conceded to be the most significant safeguard yet contrived to check excesses in administrative action.

CHAPTER IV

AGENCY JURISDICTION

The legislature initially determines the scope of an administrator's authority through the organic act by which it creates the agency. Thus, the determination of whether agency action is authorized should begin with an examination of the enabling legislation spelling out the agency's function and process.

Even at its zenith, the nondelegation doctrine did not restrict administrative agency jurisdiction "of the subject matter." Consequently, the scope of an agency's *substantive* mandate is frequently very broad. The FTC may enjoin any unfair trade practice in commerce; the NLRB is empowered to prosecute all unfair labor practices. (And what is "unfair" is essentially for the agency to decide.) All administrators do not have sweeping authority, however. Agencies assigned narrower, more specific tasks, for example, are those deciding claims and assigning benefits (social security), supervising occupational licensure (physicians to plumbers), or approving rates and routes (transportation, communication and energy supplies). Hence, the social security administrator must rule on benefit eligibility and authorize claims in accordance with standards and payment schedules set by Congress.

Within the confines of its substantive authority, the agency has a wide range of choice and can seek compliance by informal or formal action. Which alternative the administrator selects depends in part on *procedural* requirements and options. Here the administrator's authority is generally influenced by administrative law doctrines often vaguely codified in statutes of general applicability such as the APA.

A. PRIMARY JURISDICTION

The administrator who issues the license is also, in many cases, the same governmental official who makes the *initial determination* that the same license should be revoked (or suspended, renewed or, in other cases, issued). It is not for a court to decide the question first. The court may review the administrative decision; but the court's decision should come only after the agency has had an opportunity to rule. This doctrine, which carries the label of "primary jurisdiction," seeks to preserve the agency's jurisdiction over its assigned subject.

Primary jurisdiction does not necessarily determine who may begin the action in the sense of who may file a complaint against a licensee asserting that its license should be revoked. Rather, it directs where or before whom the complaint should be filed and who should first decide whether or not the license should be continued. Nor is it accurate to say that the doctrine determines whether the matter must first be submitted to an administrative agency. As a judge-made doctrine it merely guides a court in deciding whether it should consider the matter at that time or refrain until the agency with possible jurisdiction has had an opportunity to act.

In most situations it is relatively simple to decide whether a court should invoke the doctrine of primary jurisdiction and defer its consideration of the matter until the agency has had an opportunity to act. Among the easier examples where primary jurisdiction—perhaps a more descriptive term would be "initial agency jurisdiction"—applies are the SEC's power to suspend broker-dealer registration or trading on the stock market, and the CAB's allocation of airline routes or approval of air fares.

The borderland area where the doctrine's application is most frequently an issue lies in agency jurisdiction over regulated industries. Two cases involving the ICC's jurisdiction illustrate the doctrine's broad outlines. In the first, Texas & Pacific Ry. v. Abilene Cotton Oil Co., 204 U.S. 426, 27 S.Ct. 350 (1907), a shipper contended that the railroad's published rate was unreasonable and sued the railroad in court for "the excess" collected. Under the Interstate Commerce

Act, rates had to be approved by the ICC. But
the statute also allowed shippers injured by "unreasonable" rates either to complain to the ICC
or to sue in court for "the excess" paid. Despite
this rather clear statutory grant of concurrent
jurisdiction to the agency and the courts, the
Supreme Court held that "a shipper seeking rep-
aration predicated upon the unreasonableness of
the established rate must . . . primarily invoke redress" through the ICC. The ruling was
justified on practical grounds. Uniform rates
could never be achieved if they could be altered
by the decisions of judges or juries in disparate
jurisdictions as well as by the ICC; unless court
actions were curbed, preferential rates, which
were the antithesis of the congressional goal,
would result.

Then in Great Northern Ry. v. Merchants Ele-
vator Co., 259 U.S. 285, 42 S.Ct. 477 (1922), the
Court developed the concept further—even
though it was found to be inapplicable in that
case. Here Justice Brandeis observed that when
an agency possesses expertise on the disputed issue and this knowledge is not shared by the
courts, the courts should defer to the specialist.
This meant in *Great Northern*, where a shipper
and carrier disagreed over which of two conflicting portions of the railroad's rate schedule should

govern a grain shipment, that the issue did not
have to be deferred to the ICC because "what
construction shall be given to a railroad tariff
presents ordinarily a question of law which does
not differ in character from those presented
when the construction of any other document is
in dispute." And on questions of law, the courts
rather than the agencies are the experts. On the
other hand, if the "determination is reached ordinarily upon voluminous and conflicting evidence, for the adequate appreciation of which ac-
quaintance with many intricate facts of transportation is indispensable," that knowledge "is
commonly to be found only in a body of experts,"
namely the agency. Note how this law-fact distinction applied in judicial review of administrative action also governs application of the doctrine
of primary jurisdiction. That is, although courts
generally defer to agency findings of fact and inferences, they will more freely substitute their interpretations of statutes and precedents.

These foundational cases illustrate several fac-
ets of the doctrine of primary jurisdiction. First,
it is a *one-way doctrine* protecting only the agency's jurisdiction. It is applied by a court to stay
or dismiss a proceeding before it until the agency
can act upon the matter; it is not applied by
agencies or courts to defer or dismiss agency ac-

tion until a court has decided a question *—even if the doctrine ordinarily would not be invoked if the case had been presented first to a court. Second, the doctrine only allocates *jurisdictional priority*. Once the agency renders its decision, recourse to the courts—that is, judicial review of agency action—is still available. Primary jurisdiction, in brief, does not assign exclusive jurisdiction between courts and agencies; it is only one of several techniques used to set an appropriate time for judicial review. Third, the principal justification for the doctrine of primary jurisdiction is to *coordinate* the work of agencies and courts. Their activities are most likely to come into conflict where the agency's regulation is pervasive and coordinated interpretations are necessary to assure effective regulation. Thus, where uniformity is a goal, the doctrine instructs the courts to funnel the case to the supervisory agency. However, application of the doctrine does not assure uniformity or prevent agency inconsistency. Reviewing courts do not always interpret legal questions or identify fact questions identically. Nor does the Supreme Court resolve every conflict among the circuits. On the other hand, primary jurisdiction is designed to avoid major conflicts. In addition, questions

---

* The one case to the contrary, California v. FPC, 369 U.S. 482, 82 S.Ct. 901 (1962), seems erroneous. See p. 63 infra.

of technical fact, especially those involving "voluminous and conflicting facts," usually are more appropriate for specialized agencies; legal issues generally are the preserve of the courts. The doctrine of primary jurisdiction is designed to take advantage of whatever contribution the agency can make within its area of specialization. It also seems true that allowing the agency the first opportunity to decide an issue (or case) has the practical effect of giving the agency the final, or at least the controlling, voice in most cases.

Typically, these general principles are easier to state than to apply. The primary jurisdiction quandry is illustrated by another case involving the ICC, namely United States v. Western Pacific R. R., 352 U.S. 59, 77 S.Ct. 161 (1956). Here also a railroad rate was involved. The railroad had one rate for "incendiary bombs" and another (lower) rate for gasoline shipped in steel drums. The disputed shipment consisted of bomb casings filled with napalm but without the insertion of triggering fuses necessary to complete the bomb. The railroad, of course, charged the higher, bomb rate; the shipper contended that the gas drum rate should apply since, without fuses, the bombs were no more dangerous than other gas drum shipments. Notice how the primary jurisdiction precedent

of *Great Northern* could be used by either party.
On the one hand, the doctrine of primary jurisdiction appeared inappropriate (making the problem indistinguishable from *Great Northern*); the
dispute involved the meaning of a term in a tariff
and therefore called for only the familiar judicial
task of applying a broad term to a new fact situation. Moreover, uniformity of rates, the concern
of *Texas & Pacific*, was not in issue. In fact, neither the parties nor the lower court—nor the
agency—sought to apply the doctrine of primary
jurisdiction. On the other hand, *Great Northern*
also noted that primary jurisdiction is in the agency whenever significant agency expertise is involved. If bomb casings, without fuses, must be
handled like armed explosives, the "incendiary
bomb" rates should apply; if such casings can be
treated like gas drums, the lower rate should govern. Since the ICC has an intimate knowledge of railroad operations and costs, it is in the
best position to determine which handling procedure is appropriate for napalm filled bomb casings,
and therefore which rate is proper. How can a
court know which view the agency had in mind in
approving the rate? The Supreme Court was
persuaded by the need for agency expertise, holding that primary jurisdiction was in the ICC.*

* Ironically, on remand the ICC did not rely upon its expert knowledge of railroading to determine which rate applied; rather, it used the "judicial" reasoning of the low-

The most troublesome area in applying the doctrine of primary jurisdiction has proven to be that concerned with cases involving the antitrust laws. For clarification, some background is necessary here. In adopting the antitrust laws, which have general application to all business practices, Congress sought to protect the public interest by assuring competition. It reasoned that if competition were free the purchaser would, as a result have a choice of quality goods and services at the lowest reasonable price. To enforce this antitrust principle, actions to eliminate restraints on competition can be brought in the district courts (and partial concurrent jurisdiction is also given the FTC). However, administrative regulation conflicts with basic antitrust principles, for administrative regulation assumes that monopoly may be, and indeed often is, necessary. This substitutes government regulation for market forces to assure competitive benefits. (The regulatory agency is granted authority to allocate markets, to fix prices, to determine choice and quality of service, etc.) On the other hand, most, but not all, administrative regula-

er court and concluded that traditionally a tariff covering an article by its usual name applies even though shipped without all of its parts.   309 I.C.C. 249 (1959). This has led some to wonder whether the doctrine of primary jurisdiction in fact leads unnecessarily to circuitous action.

tion is incomplete; it relies upon a mixture of competition and regulation.

Thus, where a natural economic monopoly exists—for example, local gas, electric, water, or telephone service—the inherent assumption is that the service can be provided at a lower cost, and more conveniently, by one firm than by several. The function of regulation here is to protect the public from exploitation. Generally in these services there is little room for antitrust to operate. That is, the agency not only has primary jurisdiction over the industries, but also is usually granted exclusive jurisdiction to determine antitrust questions. In this context there is seldom any attempt to assert that the antitrust laws apply to the activities of these firms while they operate in the regulated sphere, and few questions of primary jurisdiction arise.

Although transportation and communications regulation originated for the purpose of control of monopoly, the antitrust laws now have only limited application to these industries. The CAB has broad powers to control air fares, the quality of passenger service, and entry into or exit from the airline bussiness—including mergers between various airlines or between airlines and other businesses. The ICC has similar powers over railroads and trucking, as does the FCC over wire or radio communication. Ocean shipping is

similarly regulated by the Federal Maritime
Commission (except that the FMC does not limit entry or exit from this business and its rate-
setting powers are less extensive). Yet, these
industries are not free of competition. For example, airlines (regulated by the CAB) compete
with each other, as well as with railroads and
trucking (supervised by the ICC) for cargo traf-
fic. Competition therefore retains a significant
place in the regulatory scheme. Nevertheless,
primary jurisdiction may apply. The relevant
regulatory statute often expressly immunizes
agreements approved by the agency from the
antitrust laws. In this situation, even if the
agency does not have the power to bind the antitrust court, the agency has primary jurisdiction
to approve the challenged conduct.

> Uniformity and consistency in the regula-
> tion of business entrusted to a particu-
> lar agency are secured, and the limited
> functions of review by the judiciary are more
> rationally exercised, by preliminary resort for
> ascertaining and interpreting the circum-
> stances underlying legal issues to agencies
> that are better equipped than courts by spe-
> cialization, by insight gained through ex-
> perience, and by more flexible procedure.
> . . . The same considerations of admin-
> istrative expertise apply, whoever initiates

the action. (Far East Conference v. United States, 342 U.S. 570, 574–76, 72 S.Ct. 492, 494–95 (1952).)

Where the regulation is pervasive, the Supreme Court has even suggested that administrative regulation may completely supersede the antitrust laws. Note, this result goes beyond the doctrine of primary jurisdiction in that the agency's jurisdiction is then total and exclusive. By immunizing the business activity (such as price-fixing, merger agreements, etc.) from the antitrust laws, even the reviewing court must accept the agency's determination as long as the other requirements of review are met. The question in this context becomes, "is this what Congress intended?" Where the antitrust issue is difficult to assess because of the regulatory context, the court will defer to the agency having comprehensive responsibility for the industry. On the other hand, once the agency determines that it has not approved (and immunized) past conduct, the antitrust court's jurisdiction with respect to that past conduct (but not to future injunctions) remains intact.

Other industries such as pipelines, broadcasters, banks and stock exchanges, are subject to a less comprehensive regulatory scheme—at least from an antitrust point of view. Here approval of its actions by the regulatory agency will not necessarily immunize the regulated firm from the antitrust laws. For example, banks are subject to extensive regulation. In connection with a merger between two banks, however, the banking agencies examine only whether the merger adversely affects the availability of banking services in the community and the financial stability of the two banks. But service and financial stability are not the primary criteria for determining the lawfulness of mergers under the antitrust laws. Consequently, the Supreme Court has held that banking regulators do not have the power to immunize bank mergers from the antitrust laws. However, primary jurisdiction still applies where the agency must give approval. This assures that the merger meets the "banking" tests.

These "limited regulation" industries have spawned separate, and sometimes conflicting, results in the application of the doctrine of primary jurisdiction. Congress has stepped in to provide that bank mergers are now subject to a special statutory approval procedure which allocates primary jurisdiction to the administrative agency and limits the scope of judicial review. On the other hand, the SEC exercises only peripheral regulation of the stock exchanges; it has no opportunity to consider antitrust aspects of regulated market activity. Consequently, denial by the exchanges of trading information and rights is subject to immediate antitrust scrutiny. It follows, therefore, that when the challenged business activity need not be approved by the agency—that is, the agency lacks authority to disapprove the action—the doctrine has no application and the court is free to exercise its jurisdiction. There is one surprising and aberrant case in this area, however, where the Supreme Court inverted the doctrine and then applied it to require the FPC to delay consideration of a pipeline merger application until an antitrust court could rule upon the merger's legality. California v. FPC, 369 U.S. 482, 82 S.Ct. 901 (1962). This result, granting a district court initial exclusive jurisdiction, is contrary to the function and purpose of the primary jurisdiction doctrine and seems unlikely to be followed.

B. RES JUDICATA

In contrast to the concept of primary jurisdiction, which protects an agency's substantive jurisdiction, application of res judicata principles in the administrative process is designed to inhibit retroactive regulation. Changing regulatory rules after the parties have relied upon them is unfair and ultimately would destroy effective regulation. Where the administrative process is similar to a court trial, agencies are generally bound by the traditional doctrine of res judicata. The agency cannot relitigate a previously decided issue with the same party. No matter how egregious the error of fact or law, the interest in ending the adjudication usually bars the parties from pressing the same claims. In the past there was some dispute over whether the judicial, common law doctrines applied; but in recent years courts have looked past labels and acknowledged that unless there is an overriding interest present which the agency is assigned to protect, res judicata principles govern administrative procedures. The difficulty, of course, lies in identifying when an agency may reinspect a prior decision. Several categories can be identified.

An agency, like a court, is free to reexamine a rule of general applicability. For example, it may rely on a technique for determining a new rate base differing from that previously utilized in setting a carrier's rates. While res judicata principles can be said to be inapplicable because a rate-order is a legislative order looking to the future and not an adjudicative order looking to the past (and res judicata principles do not apply to nonjudicial functions), the true reason for permitting the new rate, based on a new approach, is that rates are not designed to last forever and ratemaking procedures are not immutable. That is, the policy design of seeking repose, which underlies res judicata, does not apply to prospective rate orders.

This does not mean that an administrative agency can rewrite its prior orders and apply them retroactively. Parties must be able to rely upon established rate orders; thus, reparations generally cannot be awarded against charges made at previously approved rates (unless they are "unreasonable," see p. 53 supra). The same principles usually apply to money judgments issued by agencies. For example, the NLRB cannot correct a back pay award retroactively once its decision is final and the time for appeal has expired. On the other hand, the administrative statute may "notify" the parties that the administrator's order is subject to retroactive change. It is not uncommon for workmen's compensation statutes to permit administrative changes in the amount awarded the injured workman as his physical condition changes— even though a common law court could only award a lump sum payment in a similar situation. Administrative flexibility in applying res judicata principles arises most frequently in licensing situations. A license to engage in an occupation, to operate a business, or to serve specific customers or areas, can be modified or revoked if a change of conditions occurs and the public need to make the particular modification outweighs the licensee's reliance on the initial license terms—even though the license covers a specified period which has not yet expired.

More difficult, however, is the application of res judicata principles to successive complaint-type actions (those asserting law violations). For instance, just because an alien defeats one attempt to exclude or deport him, this does not mean that the government is forever barred from seeking to expel him. Yet the alien cannot be "called upon again and again to prove his right to be and remain" here. Whether the desire for repose becomes the overriding consideration depends upon many factors, in particular the type and significance of competing individual and community interests, the legislative mission of the agency, and the impact which res judicata would have on each in this situation.

For example, the FTC may prosecute a company for a false advertisement in 1972, even though the identical advertisement of the very same product was upheld under the same statute (§ 5 of the FTC Act prohibiting "unfair and deceptive trade practices") only six years earlier. See FTC v. Raladam Co., 316 U.S. 149, 62 S.Ct. 966 (1942). If the advertisement was not false in 1966, how could it be challenged *and* found to be false in 1972? The reasons are several. First, one of the major functions of the FTC is to develop the concept of false advertising to meet changing needs and conditions. If Congress could foresee all harmful business practices it would not rely upon the general language mentioned above; if it sought a static rather than an evolving law, specific limitations would have been available. Thus what is fair or at least not unfair at one time may become false at a later date (and vice versa*).

Agencies were created in part with flexibility in mind. As noted in the discussion of the nondelegation doctrine, their mandate often is to deal with problems for which only generalized rules can be supplied; the agency is charged with exploring solutions, with changing the level of acceptable practices, and with supplying specifics as experience and knowledge are developed. (The strict application—or extension—of common law rules of merger, bar or collateral estoppel would only impede this development.) Second, no significant harm is suffered by a respondent whose advertisements are challenged twice in six years. FTC orders only apply pro-

---

* Compare Cigarette Advertising Guides, reprinted 29 Fed.Reg. 8,374 (1964), with FTC Report to Congress on Cigarette Advertising (1967) (recommendation 3), reprinted 113 Cong.Rec. Pt. 15, p. 20,050–52 (1967), where the FTC first condemned and then recommended disclosure of the tar and nicotine content in cigarette advertising. Similar problems plague other agencies (e. g., FDA regulation of fat labeling of foods, circa 1959–71).

spectively. There is no penalty for past violations (until an order is entered). Nor is this FTC action a harassment. A finding of innocence does not immunize conduct forever. Third, a respondent's interest in advertising his product without limitation is insubstantial when compared to the public's interest in eliminating deceptive advertising. Community values outweigh private pecuniary interests based upon profits derived from consumer misunderstanding. Fourth, even technical common law rules of res judicata probably are inapplicable, where, although the parties and issues are identical, the time period for which the violation is claimed in the second action does not correspond to the time period of the first suit.

In summary, therefore, the judicial doctrine of res judicata will be applied to administrative hearings to prevent an agency from relitigating a question where the interest in repose is dominant, such as the adjudication of past facts. However, its application is relaxed when the issues involve law or policy and their reconsideration does not violate basic fairness standards. Although presented here as a restriction on an agency's initial jurisdiction, the issue also involves the effect or impact of a prior agency or judicial decision.

C. DISCRETION

Most agency enabling statutes authorize agency action, few compel it. In general, the legislature delegates to the administrator not only jurisdiction over the subject matter but also broad discretion in determining whether he will in fact supervise or regulate the activity and, if so, how he should proceed.

For example, the FTC has jurisdiction over "unfair and deceptive trade practices . . . in commerce." Yet it does not follow automatically that the Commission will or must prosecute every possible violation within the furthest reach of the "in commerce" jurisdiction. Whether and who to prosecute is within the agency's sound discretion. A private party may not bring an action before the FTC or a court. Nor does the enabling legislation require the Commission to enforce the FTC Act in any particular way. The FTC is not required to proceed by issuing a formal complaint and by giving the respondent an opportunity to explain his conduct in a formal trial-type hearing. Rather, the FTC may regulate by informal as well as formal means; it may seek to regulate all businesses, an industry, or only one firm. These choices in fact are often combined. Among the methods relied upon by the FTC are: policy announcements publicized by press releases; informal assurances of voluntary compliance (nonbinding agreements usually from those who have sought in good faith to comply); advisory opinions (nonbinding opinions in response to a business information request before proposed action is taken); formal consent decrees (binding final orders which do not require either an admission or a finding of guilt); broad trade regulation rules (rules adopted after formal proceedings which spell out in advance unlawful business practices—such as door-to-door sales techniques); narrower industry guides (rules dealing with a variety of problems in an industry and adopted after informal conferences with an industry—such as the cigarette advertising guides); * and, of course, formal adjudications (involving a complaint, discovery, a trial-type hearing, and an adjudicative determination of whether the law was violated and what order is necessary). While other agency procedures differ—for example, a shipper's complaint to the ICC may require the ICC to investigate—the above listing, along with its range, are typical.

Broad agency discretion is both a strength and weakness of the administrative process. On one hand, the administrator is given great flexibili-

---

* Industry guides, however, may cover general business practices such as the guides against "bait" advertising and deceptive pricing.

ty. He can select the "weapon" best suited to obtain the congressional objective. Even if he misses the mark, the costs of a mistake can be reduced. On the other hand, broad discretion can mask arbitrary and unreasonable choices. Discriminatory treatment and rule by administrator whim rather than consistent, even-handed justice, can become the routine of agency action. As the functions of administrative agencies have been broadened and their services increased— with the citizen having fewer alternatives— abuses of discretion, even if slight, become more costly in terms of effective regulation and public acceptance. This explains, in part, the growing concern of legislators, administrators, scholars and practitioners with "discretionary injustice." During the New Deal era when many agencies were created and administrative law came to prominence, the primary concern was to assure that the administrative agency had adequate powers to meet the crisis of the Great Depression. Now that agencies are assured of enough power, the present felt need and current focus is to structure and channel administrative discretion—namely, to avoid abuse without impairing agency performance.

Agencies, like district attorneys, have almost unlimited negative discretion. That is, they can decline to exercise jurisdiction even though the

matter is within the scope of their legislative
mission. The reason is simple and practical. All
regulatory authority overshoots the mark to
some extent. Not every violation can (or probably should) be punished. Law enforcement and
regulation works by example and deterrence as
well as by punishment. Self-regulation relies
primarily on adequate reporting with administrative spot checks. Moreover, agency resources
are limited; administrative agencies do not command the highest budgetary priority. When
resources are limited, sound administration requires that they be allocated rationally by the
administrator assigned the regulatory task.

There are occasional exceptions, especially in
the administration of the labor laws. For example, the Supreme Court has held that the
NLRB cannot refuse to exercise its jurisdiction
over union employers or the hotel industry. And
the Secretary of Labor has been required either
to act upon a complaint of irregularities in a contested union election or to delineate and make
explicit the basis on which discretionary nonac-
tion is taken. DeVito v. Shultz, 300 F.Supp.
381 (D.C.D.C.1969); see Medical Comm. For
Human Rights v. SEC, 432 F.2d 659 (D.C.Cir.
1970), vacated as moot, 92 S.Ct. 577 (1972).
However, these limitations on the administrator's negative discretion are, as yet, restricted

to only a few areas and are likely to have only a marginal effect on an administrator's refusal to act.

Another area of restraint is the limitation imposed upon the administrator's discretion in taking affirmative action. While a court generally cannot (or will not) tell an administrator who to regulate or prosecute, it may hold that a particular respondent cannot be singled out for "special" treatment. In FTC v. Universal-Rundle Corp., 387 U.S. 244, 87 S.Ct. 1622 (1967), the Court set forth the standard: the administrative decision to prosecute will be reversed or stayed, even if the respondent is admittedly guilty, if that decision "constitute[s] a patent abuse of discretion." What represents a patent abuse of discretion is not at all clear, however. Up to now this limitation on affirmative action has been successfully exploited only by persons who have been able to demonstrate systematic administrative discrimination. For example, in the landmark decision of Yick Wo. v. Hopkins, 118 U.S. 356, 6 S.Ct. 1064 (1886), the conviction of a laundry operator for violating a municipal health and building code was overturned upon a showing that the ordinance was being administered so that only Chinese laundries could be guilty; it was an obviously discriminatory attempt to eliminate them as business competitors. The Court did not decide, however, that the prosecution was selective (e. g., by enforcing the ordinance more frequently against unlicensed Chinese laundries than against unlicensed Caucasian laundries). When challenging a prosecutor's selection of whom to proceed against, it is practically impossible to demonstrate convincingly that the prosecutor has acted arbitrarily.

Recently, applications of the principle that affirmative agency action is subject to some outside restraint has focused on the necessity for an administrator to articulate standards and set forth reasons for his decision.* In requiring the agency to consider and then spell out why it acted in the manner it has, it is felt (perhaps it is more accurate to say, hoped) that the administrator is less likely to act arbitrarily or to favor partisan interests. Thus, in Hornsby v. Allen, 326 F.2d 605 (5th Cir. 1964), a state liquor commission was held to have violated a store owner's constitutional right to due process because it had denied her application for a license without setting forth definite rules containing standards governing license applications, and because it had failed to give the applicant any explanation for denying her particular application. Similar reasoning was relied upon in Holmes v. New York City Housing Authority, 398 F.2d 262 (2d Cir. 1968),

---

* These rulings, of course, carry forward the *DeVito* court's approach to limit agency action as well as inaction.

to require a public housing authority to develop fair, systematic procedures to process tenant applications. In Environmental Defense Fund, Inc. v. Ruckelshaus, 439 F.2d 584 (D.C.Cir.1971), the court required the administrator to rely upon a formal rulemaking hearing to rule on the safety of DDT rather than upon an informal investigation (which might unfairly favor entrenched private interests). It seems safe to predict that we have seen only the first developments in what will be a rapidly expanding area of administrative law. See also United States v. Bryant, 442 F.2d 775 (D.C. Cir. 1971). But see Jarecha v. Immigration & Naturalization Service, 417 F.2d 220 (5th Cir. 1969).

formal rule making
containing definite rules
standards

CHAPTER V

ACQUIRING INFORMATION: INVESTIGATIONS

Without information, administrative agencies could not regulate industry, protect the environment, prosecute fraud, collect taxes, or issue grants. Most administrative actions (including much of that which occurs in an informal as well as in a formal proceeding) is conditioned by the information obtained through the agency's prior investigation. Necessary information is frequently available from the staff, the agency's accumulated records, and private sources willing to divulge what they know. If these resources prove inadequate, the administrator may seek further information by summoning witnesses or documents for examination or by conducting searches.

Whatever the legitimate demands of government regulation for access to information, the Fourth Amendment's strictures against unreasonable search and seizure embody a countervailing interest of privacy. Freedom from unnecessary governmental inquisition and intrusion is both an article of faith and a necessary element of liberty in an ordered, democratic society—and even (or, perhaps, more especially) in a "welfare state." Consequently, administrative agencies do not have unrestricted power to demand information merely for satisfying their curiosity. The agency's command can be enforced only if it is authorized by law and issued in a lawful manner—in other words, if it is within the administrator's delegated powers. More importantly, constitutional limitations hedge administrative power to investigate.

But, on the other hand, ill-considered agency action could result in wasted public funds and energies, as well as in grave consequences to private parties. The mere filing of a complaint by a government agency can have severe repercussions. In this respect, the acquisition of information by an agency is necessary for protection of private interests. For example, before the SEC brings a complaint against an insider for misusing his position, it must first determine that a violation has probably occurred.

A. AUTHORITY TO INVESTIGATE

The authority to investigate is intertwined with the objectives of administrative investigation. The purposes of investigations vary, ranging over the entire spectrum of agency activity. If an agency is charged with enforcing a statute, its investigations may lay the groundwork for detecting violations and punishing wrongdoers. Thus, the Labor Department may seek to inspect an employer's payroll records when checking for compliance with minimum wage laws. However, most administrative activity does not focus directly on prosecutorial law enforcement. Investigations constitute the major tool of administrative supervision. For example, the nation's banks are supervised by the Federal Reserve Board and the Federal Deposit Insurance Corporation through visits by their inspectors for examination of the banks' records, and not through prosecution. The SEC relies primarily upon compulsory disclosure to regulate securities fraud. Agencies regulating transportation, pipelines and communications have employed investigations for development of information for formulating policy or rules. Their studies into youth fares, electricity shortages, and television commercials aimed at children are recent examples. Similarly, before it recommended congressional legislation for regulation of cigarette packaging and advertising, the FTC held several public hearings to permit interested persons to air their views and submit information. Sometimes administrative investigations seek merely to illuminate areas previously obscured. The Civil Rights Commission has relied upon public investigation to call attention to discriminatory practices which were earlier hidden from public view. Frequently, these informational investigations have led to proposals for corrective legislation and new programs.

Because the administrative need for information varies widely, and often is unpredictable,

[78]

Congress has traditionally conferred broad powers of investigation upon the agencies. Significant and typical (its provisions having been repeated in almost every agency enabling act adopted since 1914) are the provisions of the FTC Act (15 U.S.C.A. §§ 46, 49), empowering the Commission to (1) direct corporations to file annual or special reports and answer specific questions in writing; (2) obtain access to corporate files for examination and reproduction of their contents; and (3) subpoena the attendance of witnesses and the production of documentary evidence. Congress would be hard-pressed to devise a broader authorization. This does not mean that agencies can coerce any information. But if the agency is persistent and careful, there is little beyond its reach.

Despite this broad mandate, agency investigations at one time were severely restricted. Courts initially held that an agency could not compel testimony for informational (in contrast to regulatory, i. e., law enforcement) purposes unless specifically authorized by the legislature. When this authority was delegated to the agencies, the courts switched their ground, and asserted that "fishing expeditions" which sought to inspect corporate records merely to determine whether "something will turn up," violated the spirit and letter of the Fourth Amendment; that is, the search was unreasonable when the agency failed to show probable cause that a violation had occurred or had not framed its demand in specific terms.   FTC v. American Tobacco Co., 264 U.S. 298, 44 S.Ct. 336 (1924) (Holmes, J.).

As the Supreme Court perceived that written records were not only the mainstay of modern corporate operations but also the major tool for acquiring reliable data and for assuring compliance with the law (most noncriminal law enforcement—e. g., tax collection—relies upon self-reporting), it modified its stance.   First in Endicott Johnson Corp. v. Perkins, 317 U.S. 501, 63 S.Ct. 339 (1943), the Court eliminated the "probable cause" standard when it upheld an agency subpoena, even though the agency did not show that the company whose records were sought was subject to the agency's jurisdiction—or even, probable jurisdiction.   Then in Oklahoma Press Publ. Co. v. Walling, 327 U.S. 186, 66 S.Ct. 494 (1946), the Court applied a standard of reasonableness to the requirement of particularity; the "specification of the documents to be produced [must be] adequate, but not excessive, for the purposes of the relevant inquiry."   Holmes' nostalgic dictum was finally laid to rest in 1950 when the Supreme Court commented: "Even if one were to regard the request for information in this case as caused by nothing more than official curiosity, nevertheless law-enforcing agencies have a legitimate right to satisfy themselves that corporate behavior is consistent with the law and the public interest." United States v. Morton Salt Co., 338 U.S. 632, 652, 70 S.Ct. 357, 369 (1957).

In the succeeding years the courts have fleshed out the legitimate boundaries of administrative investigation and required that:

1. *The investigation must be authorized by law and "conducted pursuant to a legitimate purpose."* 5 U.S.C.A. § 555(c), (d); United States v. Powell, 379 U.S. 48, 85 S.Ct. 248 (1964). An administrator cannot confer power on himself; his subpoena need not be obeyed unless he has authority to summon the witness or information. Nor may the investigative power be used as a club to harass. However, if the administrator establishes an apparently valid need for the information, the burden of showing abuse of investigative power is on the accuser.

2. *The information sought must be relevant to a lawful subject of investigation.* United States v. Powell, supra. In determining whether the information is relevant, the administrator may be required to reveal the purpose of his inquiry. But during the course of an investigation it may not be possible to determine precisely whether evi-

dence is germane.   Consequently, "[o]nly where the futility of the process to uncover anything legitimate is inevitable or obvious must there be a halt upon the threshold." Matter of Edge Ho Holding Corp., 256 N.Y. 374, 382, 176 N.E. 537, 539 (1931) (Cardozo, C. J.).   Again, the burden of establishing irrelevance is upon the person objecting to the subpoena.

3.   *The investigative demand must be reasonable.* Specifically, the administrator must identify the information requested with as much particularity as possible, and the burden imposed by the request must not outweigh possible benefits of the administrative purpose.   As a practical matter, administrative commands are denied only where the request is extreme or unnecessarily vague or oppressive.   In addition, trade secrets and other confidential information cannot be kept from agency scrutiny.   Protective orders are not uncommon, however.   Practical accommodations, such as allowing a person to supply documents at his office and over a period of time, are not unusual, especially when the subpoena is served upon a nonparty.   Yet the Fourth Amendment has been applied to limit physical inspections (discussed further at pp. 87–90, infra).

4. *The information sought cannot be summoned if it is privileged.* Most of the controversy surrounding this limitation has been concerned with the scope of the self-incrimination privilege located in the Fifth Amendment. The extent of this protection is considered in the next section. The option of remaining silent is also applicable in cases involving testimonial privilege recognized in the law of evidence—e. g., where there exist doctor-patient, lawyer-client, husband-wife relationships. Although agency statutes and regulations are silent on the point, the courts have assumed that agency proceedings are subject to the same privileges as judicial proceedings. E. g., McMann v. SEC, 87 F.2d 377, 378 (2d Cir. 1937) (Hand, J.).

Finally, it should be noted that the present route for enforcement of an agency's investigatory powers is a two-step process. When the respondent refuses to produce the information, the agency must first apply for a judicial order of compliance. Then, if the judicial order is ignored, the respondent is subject to contempt. This procedure enables private parties to obtain judicial scrutiny of agency compliance with these requirements before any sanctions are applied.

[*83*]

B. SELF–INCRIMINATION

Even though administrative agencies cannot as a rule impose criminal penalties, their procedures are not exempt from constitutional limitations. The Fifth Amendment's assurance that no person "shall be compelled in any criminal case to be a witness against himself," has long been interpreted to mean that a witness in an administrative investigation (as well as in an adjudicative hearing) may not be coerced to respond if his reply could either incriminate him or provide a link in a chain of evidence against him. In this situation, the witness usually fears the potential administrative order less than the subsequent use of his testimony in a criminal proceeding. This constitutional privilege applies to written documents as well as to oral testimony.

However, the self-incrimination privilege has its limitations. First, the privilege applies only to natural persons and therefore does not protect corporations and other legal entities. Since corporations cannot be given the "third degree," they need no protection from government torture.* Second, the privilege can be circumvented by the grant of immunity from criminal prose-

---

* Corporations are protected from harassment, however, since the same word "person" in the Fifth Amendment is interpreted to cover corporations and associations when the due process clause is in issue.

cution. Federal agencies have commonly been authorized to grant immunity and then to compel a witness to testify—even if the evidence might implicate or possibly expose him to "loss of job, expulsion from labor unions, state registration and investigation statutes, passport eligibility, and general public opprobrium." Ullmann v. United States, 350 U.S. 422, 430, 76 S.Ct. 497, 502 (1956). The Organized Crime Control Act of 1970 repealed most agency immunity statutes and rewrote their immunity powers. 18 U.S.C.A. § 6004. While immunity may still be granted to witnesses appearing before administrative agencies, the Attorney General's prior approval is now required. However, application of the immunity provision does not preclude the agency from issuing an order (noncriminal) against the immune witness, even though the order is based upon the incriminatory testimony.

A third, and ill-defined, limitation of the Fifth Amendment privilege arises from the administrative power to require the keeping of business records which are open to administrative inspection. For example, to aid the enforcement of World War II price controls, the Price Administrator required businessmen to keep records of the prices at which they sold their products and services. In Shapiro v. United States, 335 U.S. 1, 68 S.Ct. 1375 (1948), a wholesaler of fruit and pro-

duce presented records in compliance with a subpoena but sought refuge in statutory immunity
since the records were coerced. In upholding a
criminal prosecution of the wholesaler for violation of the Price Control Act, the Court explained that "the privilege which exists as to
private papers cannot be maintained in relation
to 'records required by law to be kept in order that
there may be suitable information of transactions
which are the appropriate subjects of governmental regulation and the enforcement of restrictions validly established.' "

However, this exception to the self-incrimination privilege has been narrowed and possibly
eliminated as a practical matter by recent Supreme Court rulings. In Marchetti v. United
States, 390 U.S. 39, 88 S.Ct. 697 (1968), and
Grosso v. United States, 390 U.S. 62, 88 S.Ct. 709
(1968), the Court upheld assertions of the privilege as a defense to criminal prosecutions for
violations of both the registration and taxing
provisions of the federal wagering statutes. The
obligation to pay taxes could not be separated
from the information revealed by the records
and incriminatory purposes of the statutes. In
order for the required records exception to apply,
the three premises of the *Shapiro* doctrine must
be met: "first, the purposes of the United States'
inquiry must be essentially *regulatory*; second,

information is to be obtained by requiring the preservation of *records* of a kind which the regulated party has *customarily kept*; and third, the records themselves must have assumed 'public aspects' which render them at least analogous to *public documents*." Whether the required records exception meaningfully extends beyond price records seems questionable.

C. PHYSICAL INSPECTIONS

Agencies also acquire information through direct observation. Administrative inspections cover a wide range of activity, including safety tests of commercial equipment and personal cars, sanitary inspections of restaurants and hotels, and fire and health checks of apartments and homes. Although occasionally used for law enforcement, their primary function is to prevent and correct undesirable conditions. They create a special concern, however, where inspections intrude upon the intensely personal area of the privacy of the home. Nevertheless, the administrative inspection does not face a blanket constitutional prohibition such as the Fifth Amendment's exclusion of coerced incriminatory statements. The Fourth Amendment exhibits a balanced concern against "unreasonable searches and seizures." In other words, a reasonable inspection would not seem to require a warrant, and any inspection is possible when a warrant has been obtained upon a showing of "probable cause"— even though the evidence may be incriminatory.

At one time a health inspector did not need a search warrant in order to enter a house in search of a source of rats in the neighborhood if the authorizing statute imposed reasonable safeguards (e. g., procedures to identify the inspector, entry only during business hours, etc.).   Frank v. Maryland, 359 U.S. 360, 79 S.Ct. 804 (1959). Limited investigations were constitutionally permissible without prior judicial authorization because the strong public interest in sanitation and the historical acceptance of such inspections outweighed the individual's interest in privacy; nor were such searches considered a threat to the individual's right of self-protection (also reflected in the Fifth Amendment) since criminal prosecution was unlikely.

However, this view was overturned in two inspection cases, Camara v. Municipal Court, 387 U.S. 523, 87 S.Ct. 1727 (1967) (apartment building), and See v. Seattle, 387 U.S. 541, 87 S.Ct. 1737 (1967) (commercial warehouse). Although routine fire and health inspections may constitute a less hostile intrusion than the typical police search for the fruits and instruments of crime, the Court reasoned that "[i]t is surely anomalous to say that the individual

[*88*]

and his private property are fully protected by the Fourth Amendment only when the individual is suspected of criminal behavior." Health and fire codes are frequently enforced by criminal processes; refusal of entry itself may be a crime. And, "even the most law-abiding citizen has a very tangible interest in limiting the circumstances under which the sanctity of his home may be broken by official authority . . . ." Consequently, the Court ruled that the Fourth Amendment applied with full force to routine administrative inspections.

On the other hand, the Supreme Court was concerned that the great public interest in effective enforcement of safety and sanitation standards might be frustrated if routine periodic inspections of all structures were impeded. The Court resolved the problem in *Camara* by departing from the traditionally inflexible notion of "probable cause" (which required a showing that a law violation had occurred). Probable cause supporting a warrant for an administrative inspection exists, the Court ruled, "if reasonable legislative or administrative standards for conducting an area inspection are satisfied . . . ." Such standards will vary with the particular program being enforced. They "may be based upon the passage of time, the nature of the building (e. g., a multi-family apartment house), or the condition of the entire area, but they will not necessarily depend upon specific knowledge of the condition of the particular dwelling."

What this open-ended standard means in practical terms is still far from clear. If warrants are issued without detailed judicial inquiry, nothing will have changed. The *Camara* decision will have merely added another formal step. On the other hand, if notice is given to the private party, the inspection is reviewed by a superior (administrative) official, and the issuing (judicial) authority reviews the necessity for the inspection, the protection afforded private parties may be significantly enhanced without unduly inhibiting administrative inspections. Yet, as has been suggested, the suppression of illegally acquired evidence is likely to produce more substantial protection than the diluted search warrant procedure authorized in *Camara* and *See*. Finally, the analysis of a four member majority of the Court in Wyman v. James, 400 U.S. 309, 91 S.Ct. 381 (1971)—upholding a state's conditional grant of welfare benefits on allowance of a periodic home visit by a caseworker—may presage a more restricted application of the Fourth Amendment (and, perhaps, a return to the *Frank* "no warrant" approach).

D. RIGHTS OF WITNESSES

Witnesses in judicial investigations generally are not entitled either to legal counsel or to the opportunity to present their case, except as it relates to the questions asked of them. Even though the "right to counsel" has been expanded considerably, this should not be surprising. A person subpoenaed by a grand jury cannot take his attorney into the grand jury room, cross-examine other witnesses or proffer rebuttal evidence.* The reason is obvious; the witness is not on "trial." The grand jury's primary purpose is to determine whether there is sufficient evidence to support a subsequent prosecution. That is, the grand jury determines whether there exists a prima facie case that a law violation occurred. The question of guilt—the weighing of all the evidence—is for the trial jury to decide; it is not the province of the grand jury. Although the witness is compelled to testify before the grand jury, the evidence is kept secret and, in any case, the testimony is usually privileged from subsequent disclosure. Consequently, in these proceedings the rights of a witness to apprisal, counsel, confrontation, and cross-examination are not

---

* The same rules apply to a witness at the trial stage where he cannot seek his attorney's advice while being interrogated; nor can he cross-examine other witnesses or present his own evidence.

available—even if he is the subject of investigation.

As long as administrative investigations parallel the grand jury model (i. e., nonpublic, nonadjudicative investigation), witnesses in agency investigations have similar rights and disabilities. For example, in Anonymous v. Baker, 360 U.S. 287, 79 S.Ct. 1157 (1959), a witness compelled to appear before a state judge engaged in a nonpublic investigation of the alleged unethical behavior of several attorneys was not entitled to counsel. Similarly, the Court rejected (5 to 4) a constitutional claim for counsel in In re Groban, 352 U.S. 330, 77 S.Ct. 510 (1957), by a witness in a nonpublic hearing before a fire marshall for investigation of the cause of a suspicious fire.

However, failure to warn a witness of his right to remain silent and to seek counsel may be necessary in order to protect the subsequent admissibility of his statement (without grant of criminal immunity) and the later use of evidence discovered through the investigation. To date the warning required in criminal investigations by Miranda v. Arizona, 384 U.S. 436, 86 S.Ct. 1602 (1966), has been applied primarily to tax investigations which may lead to criminal charges; other administrative investigations are, in general, not criminal in nature and do not involve the "custodial" feature so critical in *Miranda*. Likewise, the wake of Gideon v. Wainwright, 372 U.S. 335, 83 S.Ct. 792 (1963), may require the appointment of counsel by agencies for indigent witnesses. As in the area of criminal procedure, however, *Gideon's* impact has been principally in connection with providing counsel at the trial stage. Even there few agencies have established procedures for appointment of counsel. Movement toward expanded rights of representation can be discerned occasionally in revocation of parole and probation proceedings. Here administrative law and criminal procedure join.

The primary difficulty with adherence to the grand jury analogue in determining the right to counsel in administrative investigations is that many do not resemble grand jury proceedings. The word "investigation" covers "such disparate practices as the inspection of factory and food processing lines by the FDA and the Department of Agriculture; inspection and copying of records by the Wage and Hour and Public Contracts Divisions of the Department of Labor; seizure and examination of mail by post-office inspectors; physical examinations of aliens; aircraft accident investigations by the CAB; and the public hearings into economic matters that may occasionally be conducted by the FTC or the SEC." Selected Reports of the Administrative Conference of the United States, S.Doc.No. 24, 88th

Cong., 1st Sess. 231 (1963). Where the object
of the investigation is informational and the witness is not likely to be implicated in wrongdoing,
the right to counsel may be of little importance
either to the witness or to the agency. On the
other hand, where the submission is voluntary
(which is the norm of administrative investigations, in contrast to that of grand juries, where
the witnesses are compelled to attend and testify) and the witness' conduct is in question, he
is likely to forfeit constitutional and testimonial
privileges such as the right against self-incrimination and the attorney-client privilege unless
properly advised. Oddly, few agencies or courts
have sought to make any distinctions among the
various types of administrative investigations in
considering the scope of the right to representation.

The slow pace of constitutional change in the
rights of witnesses in administrative investigations is partly explained by section 6(a) of the
APA which provides: "A person compelled to
appear in person before an agency or representative thereof is entitled to be accompanied, represented, and advised by counsel or, if permitted by
the agency, by other qualified representative."
5 U.S.C.A. § 555(b).* The exact meaning of

---

* One consequence is that (at least at the federal agency level) the continuing validity of *Baker* and *Groban*—
that a witness in a nonpublic investigation has no constitutional right to counsel—will not be challenged.

this APA sentence has been the subject of wide dispute. It means counsel of one's choice, but it does not apply to statements voluntarily made. While the Supreme Court has not specifically addressed itself to the scope of representation required under section 6(a) of the APA, in Hannah v. Larche, 363 U.S. 420, 80 S.Ct. 1502 (1960), it did hold that the Civil Rights Commission did not violate the due process clause when it denied voting registrars the right to cross-examine accusatory witnesses during what was technically an informational investigation—even though the registrars had been compelled to testify at public hearings and were under suspicion of violating federal law. The majority emphasized that the CRC's powers were limited to investigation, study and announcement; that it could not adjudicate. The Court's concern was that if any witness were permitted to be cross-examined by counsel for the registrars, "the investigative process could be completely disrupted . . . [and] transformed into trial-like proceedings."

Moving beyond the narrow requirements of the Constitution and the APA, the 1961–62 Administrative Conference of the United States recommended that agencies expand the right to counsel and (1) grant "voluntary" and "compelled" witnesses the same right to counsel; (2) allow counsel for a witness to make objections on

the record and to argue (briefly) the basis for
such objections; and (3) where possible, permit cross-examination and the production of limited rebuttal evidence in public investigations
implicating the witness in wrongdoing. Recommendation Nos. 15 & 25, S.Doc.No. 24, 88th
Cong., 1st Sess. 46, 54, 225 (1963). These sug-
gestions are beginning to be reflected in agency
practice.

E. PUBLICITY AND CONFIDENTIALITY

Intimately related with the issue of the right
to counsel is the right of the witness to have the
entire investigation kept private, the disclosure
of confidential information limited, and the release of damaging or defamatory material avoided. The type (public or private) and purpose
(information or regulatory) of an administrative investigation is critical. However, one thing
is clear. No matter how sensitive the information may be, if the agency's request is authorized
and meets the requirements of relevance and
particularity (and there is no overriding statutory protection available—as with secret documents in the executive branch—or other recognized privilege), the administrator cannot be denied the material merely because it is sensitive.

On the other hand, if the witness asserts that
the requested information deserves confidential

treatment, that request is invariably honored (i. e., the information is given *in camera* or secretly) unless the investigation is a public informational inquiry and the public interest in disclosure cannot otherwise be satisfied. Generally there is no particular need for public disclosure of sensitive information where the investigation is private or where, even if public, a subsequent trial is expected if wrongdoing is found. The public character of a trial is designed to keep the judge and the witness fair and honest. The accused—the person most likely to be injured by public disclosure—can minimize any harm to himself by cross-examining witnesses and by presenting his own case. The rights of the occasional witness who may be injured by any disclosure must give way to the predominant interest of protecting the accused and focusing the trial issues on his conduct. Since pretrial investigations cannot lead to official sanctions, the credibility of witnesses and the fairness of an examiner's rulings are not generally subject to challenge. Consequently, an investigated party's right to counsel is limited. It follows, a fortiori, that while the public interest in disclosure weighs heavily after it has been found that probable cause exists (namely, at the trial stage), no such counterbalance is present during the precomplaint investigation. But see Hannah v. Larche,

363 U.S. 420, 80 S.Ct. 1502 (1960). However, if
the investigation is a broad economic or informational inquiry, the standard for confidentiali-
ty conforms more closely to that in adjudicative
hearings. There is a strong public interest in
making all information public and a heavy burden is imposed on persons seeking secrecy. See
FCC v. Schreiber, 381 U.S. 279, 293–94, 85 S.Ct.
1459, 1469–70 (1965).

The difficulty in applying this standard is that
what appears to be informational to the agency
often seems inquisitorial and regulatory to the
witness. In *Hannah* the Civil Rights Commission asserted that it sought to inform the public about voting registration practices in the
South; however, the registrars viewed the proceeding as a Star Chamber where they were to
be tried by publicity. Yet the Supreme Court's
decision is not dispositive of the question, because the issue arose prior to any public hearings
and the CRC had a rule requiring that testimony
which may tend to defame or intimidate was to
be taken in executive (i. e., non-public) session.
And in Jenkins v. McKeithen, 395 U.S. 411, 89
S.Ct. 1843 (1969), the Court held that a state
statute establishing a commission to conduct public hearings and make findings about criminal
law violations in labor-management relations—
but without the power to make a binding adju-

dication—failed to meet due process requirements of confrontation and cross-examination.
The Court accepted the witness' allegation that
the function of the agency was "publicly to brand
him a criminal without trial." *

Finally, Congress amended section 3 of the
APA compelling each federal agency to make
"promptly available to any person" requested
records that he has identified. 5 U.S.C.A. § 552.
(See pp. 40–41, supra.)   If the agency refuses to
disclose the material, the requester may seek to
compel disclosure by a de novo trial in a federal
district court where, the statute specifies, "the
burden is on the agency to sustain its action."
5 U.S.C.A. § 552(a) (3). Unfortunately, the art-
less language of the statute and its exemptions,
while probably opening agency files slightly, has
created a plethora of difficult interpretative issues. The principal questions are concerned with
the limits of the various exemptions and the matter of whether there exists an equity power in
the federal courts to deny disclosure even where
no specific exemption is available. These questions have not been resolved authoritatively.

---

* However, three Justices dissented and two members
of the five member majority reaffirmed Hannah (indicating
that with the dissenters, a majority of the Court as then
constituted still approved that decision).

CHAPTER VI

INFORMAL ADMINISTRATIVE PROCESS

Although administrative law cases and materials are primarily concerned with prospective rulemaking (the formulation of policy) and retrospective adjudication (the application of policy in a trial), the great bulk of administrative decisions are reached informally and through mutual (though often coerced) consent. As one study concluded: Informal administrative procedures "are truly the lifeblood of the administrative process."

A. TESTS AND INSPECTIONS

A person seeking a driver's license must usually pass a written exam, an eyesight check, and a driving test. All of these are administered by trained inspectors (usually highway patrolmen). Reliance is not placed on formal, judicialized procedures, not because they are impossible, but because they would prove cumbersome and less accurate. A hearing officer could be designated, a trial held (with the participants sworn in, examined and cross-examined, or the tests re-run before the examiner) and a decision announced with supporting findings—but the mere description of this process evidences its futility. The applicant for a driver's license wants an immediate decision without unnecessary red tape. Formal procedures are time-consuming and unlikely to result in greater accuracy or fairness. The inspection or test is the deciding element. Oral or documentary evidence—the mainstay of formal procedures—play little or no part.

As government regulation has expanded, especially in the increased role of administrative agencies in preventing accidents and assuring product and service quality, the administrative process has tended to rely increasingly upon informal tests. Informal inspections determine whether cars, planes and trains can move, agricultural products can meet quality standards, periodicals can obtain second class mailing privileges, etc. Reliance is placed upon similar procedures to prevent the distribution of unsafe foods and drugs, to prohibit the entry of diseased plants and animals, or to suspend the license of a pilot pending a disciplinary hearing. Where a product is involved, it is usually impounded and frequently destroyed. When there are other overriding public interests, additional reasons exist for accepting the inspector's on-the-spot analysis. Just as the common law permitted summary abatement of a nuisance pending a hearing, threats to the protection of public health and

safety cannot be permitted through the postponement of administrative action against an immediate menace pending the holding of a hearing.
When the FDA finds botulism in soup, the manufacturer will withdraw the product from grocers
and manufacturers shelves and destroy all cans
(because of the unstated but understood FDA
threat to prosecute otherwise). As a result, any
subsequent formal hearing disputing the FDA
decision and seeking damages can do little more
than "replay" the inspector's test—except that
in this instance the evidence may sometimes be
missing, placing the integrity of the inspector and
his test procedures directly in issue.

Consequently, the emphasis of administrative
law in such cases has been to assure that the
tests are fair and the results accurate. Pressure is on both sides to negotiate their differences. Protection is afforded by allowing, where
emergency destruction is not required, a right
of re-examination before another (and usually
independent) inspector. In addition, the skills
and integrity of the inspector are checked
through setting qualification standards for these
personnel and providing expert supervision (especially through unannounced spot-checks). On
the other hand, it was long assumed that there
was little criticism of this informal system due
to the fact that it operated so well. But dis-

turbing counter evidence has been revealed in recent years. For example, until exposed, meat-packing companies commonly paid the overtime of Department of Agriculture inspectors; and it appears that some inspectors exchanged relaxed inspection for increased overtime pay. There have been few empirical studies of the accuracy or fairness of informal administrative inspections for thirty years.

B. SUPERVISION

The constant surveillance of business activities frequently undertaken by regulatory agencies to assure compliance with their directives is similar to physical inspection of regulated products. National bank regulation, as previously noted, is probably the outstanding example of pervasive regulation by supervision instead of actual government ownership and operation of the business. Administrators determine who can enter the business and open a bank, whether a branch bank can be opened and where it can be located, what cash reserves must be maintained, what auditing procedures must be followed, whether the bank can enter other businesses or offer auxiliary services, whether it can close its doors and cease to do business, etc. The administrator is even empowered to take over a bank at his discretion and without a prior hearing in order to protect its creditors. Fahey v. Mallonee, 332 U.S. 245, 67 S.Ct. 1552 (1947). Adherence to this extensive regulatory framework is enforced by daily supervision and periodic (often unannounced) visits by bank examiners. Because of the delicate nature of public confidence in the banking business (it is impossible to operate a bank once its soundness is publicly questioned by an administrative regulator) deviations are usually resolved quietly by mutual consent. Professor Davis accurately summarizes the process this way: "Adjudication gives way almost entirely to supervision. The administrative mainstay is prevention rather than cure or punishment. The sanction is not the power of suspension but the institution of proceedings." 1 K. C. Davis, Administrative Law Treatise § 4.04, at 249 (1958). Thus, the concern is with the development of methods of procedural fairness without necessitating resort to formal adjudication. Notice of an alleged deficiency and an opportunity to present the banks' views—in private —appear to be the procedural trend.

The SEC's "no action" letter provides another illustration. Technically these letters advise stockholders whether they must register a stock in order to sell it without risking SEC enforcement action; practically they advise the holder whether the issue falls within the "private offering" exemption. Seldom is there any prospect of SEC prosecution. The regulation is nevertheless effective because of the potential absolute liability of selling shareholders to subsequent purchasers and because of broker-dealer fears of disciplinary action. Recently steps have been taken to assure that the Commission and its staff do not act arbitrarily in refusing no action letters by making such letters publicly available. The assumption is that if the agency must disclose the reasons for its actions, it will be less likely to discriminate in its issue of no action letters.

Constant surveillance may serve another function—that of making an agency's negotiation and settlement procedure effective. Where the industry is complex and the information needed is sophisticated, the parties (the regulating agency and the regulated industry) must have equal access to all relevant data. In the telephone industry, the FCC has established extensive reporting requirements for interstate telephone companies (90% of which are part of the Bell System). The resulting open availability of the data necessary for establishing telephone rates has meant that the FCC has resorted to formal complaints in only two proceedings in the first 29 years of its jurisdiction over long-distance telephone rates. Even then, the rates were established informally before the rate hearings were completed.* Routine reporting and disclosure has had, in this situation, the effect of continuous surveillance. It narrows the range of factual differences, thus contributing to informal settlements.

These examples illustrate a distinctive hallmark of administrative law, namely its flexibility. No single procedure is relied upon to achieve the objectives of accuracy, efficiency and fairness. One case may require a procedure for private appeals; another may need the exposure of a public record. Surveillance may be designed to assure compliance with administrative policy or to facilitate the establishment of prices at a reasonable administrative cost. Informal (versus formal) regulation is not without its limitations. Inevitably it relies upon a threat to invoke formal powers and is ineffective unless this threat is viable. More significantly, as a recent study of the FCC disclosed, this approach "although expeditious in the short run, has inhibited the development of an adequate and competent agency staff, delayed the development of an adequate methodology of regulation, and resulted in a conspicuous

---

* During this period, 22 reductions and 1 increase were negotiated. But close supervision is not necessarily the equivalent of effective regulation as the FCC's current (and sputtering) investigation of AT & T's financial structure suggests.

failure to formulate visible and conspicuous standards."

C. APPLICATIONS AND CLAIMS

Administrative agencies were often created to provide expeditious processing of a large number of claims and applications. For example, each year the FCC disposes of half a million transmitter applications, the Immigration and Naturalization Service handles a million requests, the Social Security Administration passes upon five million benefit claims, and the IRS receives over 100 million tax returns (of which it examines two and one-half million). Obviously, with all but a handful of these claims and applications the disposition must be informal. (Only about 200 of the FCC transmitter applications result in formal cases; the IRS recommends prosecution in approximately 1,000 cases but usually only 40 of these are decided formally.) No administrative system could survive if formal hearings were required in every instance. Impartial, formal procedures must be available ultimately if the parties cannot resolve their differences; however, "it is equally if not more important that the procedure for informal decision, which will affect the greater number, be swift, simple, and fair."

Administrative agencies have developed efficient informal systems. The IRS, for example, prepares forms which are relatively simple to complete, writes instruction pamphlets, provides assistance in the preparation and development of tax returns (even to the extent of computing the tax due on incomes under $20,000), and makes its personnel available to taxpayers in the field, where it makes its initial decisions (or at a central computer office) on the basis of the information supplied by the taxpayer. Only after the return has passed through this sieve of informal decision—which usually is the end of the matter—are formal proceedings considered.

D. NEGOTIATION AND SETTLEMENT

The caseload of administrative tribunals is enormous, far exceeding that of the judicial system. Agencies have responded by perfecting informal settlement and negotiation procedures. As noted in connection with long-distance telephone ratemaking, constant supervision resulting in mutual awareness of relevant data encourages informal settlement in regulated industry proceedings. Rules spelling out agency policy and its interpretation of statutory authority discourage parties from seeking formal adjudication in most situations. The distinctive aspect of the administrative agency approach **to** settlement is that consent negotiation procedures are frequently incorporated into agency rules of practice.

Section 5(b) of the APA requires agencies to give respondents in complaint cases an opportunity for settlement "when time, the nature of the proceeding, and the public interest permit." 5 U.S.C.A. § 554(c). Similarly, license applicants must be given an "opportunity to demonstrate or achieve compliance with all lawful requirements." 5 U.S.C.A. § 558(c). In complaint cases, agencies have sought to comply with this mandate either by allowing the respondent to request consideration of a settlement after the complaint has been issued or by submitting the proposed complaint (before it has been formally issued) to the respondent as the basis for consent negotiation. Whatever the procedure, it is clear that the consent order has the effect of a final agency order.* NLRB v. Ochoa Fertilizer Corp., 368 U.S. 318, 82 S.Ct. 344 (1961).

The more difficult legal question is the scope of the requirements imposed by the APA. At a minimum, it imposes a duty on the agency to consider offers of settlement or compromise.

---

* However, a consent order usually does not include an admission of material facts or of a law violation. The agency exchanges this avoidance of almost certain civil liability for the added cost savings and greater coverage of its orders.

However, the agency retains broad (but not un-limited) discretion to determine whether the set-tlement is in the public interest. Thus, the agen-cy may be reversed if it refuses to permit any settlement negotiations; however, the decision of whether to accept, reject or negotiate the set-tlement offer is generally left to the agency's un-reviewable discretion.

E. INFORMAL SANCTIONS: PUBLICITY

Perhaps the most potent (and potentially abu-sive) power in any administrator's hands—other than the power of summary seizure—is the pow-er to publicize. For example, shortly before Thanksgiving in 1959, the Secretary of HEW de-stroyed virtually the entire cranberry market by announcing at a press conference that some cran-berries were contaminated by a cancer-produc-ing agent. In retrospect it seems that the Sec-retary was in error—and Congress made partial amends to the growers (by appropriating funds to compensate growers for the "lost" 1959 crop). The power of publicity was recently confirmed by the announcement that botulism in a can of vichyssoise had killed a man; the publicity led to the bankruptcy of Bon Vivant Soup Company. In that case, however, there was no doubt that respondent's products were adulterated and subject to seizure.* Unfortunately, not all press releases are accurate and not all injured respondents have the political clout to obtain congressional redress. Nor is the power of publicity confined to food products endangering public health. Informal SEC controls applied to the securities industry rest on a universal acknowledgment that public confidence is the mainstay of any successful securities issue. Issuers of securities do not risk "stop order" proceedings if they have any plans to market the security.

The legal controls on administrative press releases are as undeveloped as the power of publicity is extensive. The government and the administrator who acts in good faith are immune from tort liability for defamation. Again, the "people's right to know" anything seemingly justifies an almost unlimited privilege. See Barr v. Matteo, 360 U.S. 564, 577, 79 S.Ct. 1335, 1342 (1959) (Black, J., concurring). Similarly, the issuance of press releases to alert the public to suspected law violations is not ultra vires. FTC v. Cinderella Career & Finishing Schools, Inc., 404 F.2d 1308 (D.C. Cir. 1968). The problem of establishing some legal controls is not insoluble,

---

* Nor is this power confined to public officials. The recent demise of the Corvair is undoubtedly the result of Ralph Nader's book, Unsafe at Any Speed (1965) and his subsequent efforts.

however. Where the agency has determined probable cause exists that the questioned activity is dangerous or harmful to the public health or safety or constitutes economic fraud, and where pretrial publicity would unfairly injure an innocent respondent, the simplest solution is to give the respondent in lieu of pretrial publicity an option to discontinue the allegedly harmful practice pending trial. The public interest is served by avoiding continued harm from the challenged practice, and the respondent is protected from adverse publicity. This solution is not perfect, however. The respondent does not discontinue the challenged practice without cost. Where the public injury inheres in the product— the "cancerous" cranberry crop, the "contaminated" beans or soup—the respondent may be faced with a Hobson's choice. Nevertheless this suggestion could be a first step in controlling administrative discretion to issue damaging press releases. This suggests that amendment of the Federal Torts Claims Act to allow recovery for unwarranted, erroneous publicity may need to be an additional alternative.

F. INFORMAL ADVICE, ADVISORY OPINIONS AND DECLARATORY ORDERS

The most frequent contact between private parties and administrators involves the seeking and giving of interpretative advice. Though courts may presume that every man knows the law, the administrator and regulated party know that laws are neither self-executing nor easily understood or applied. As laws become more complicated to meet the needs of an increasingly complex society, the greater the need for authoritative administrative interpretations which allow the parties to avoid the substantial costs of formal adjudication or rulemaking. Consequently, almost every agency has developed extensive interpretative services. At its most common and most significant (at least to the practicing attorney) level, it involves merely the answering of telephone or written inquiries. As the legal issues become more difficult—and usually of greater importance to both parties—the response is less informal.

The Internal Revenue Service's revenue ruling procedure is an outstanding example of the informal process. It issues tens of thousands of rulings annually. They are of two categories: (1) unpublished ("private") rulings issued by Branch Offices without extensive internal review; and (2) published rulings issued from the Commissioner's office. The IRS cautions, however, that private rulings should not be relied upon by other taxpayers, even if their situations are identical, since private rulings have not been given thorough consideration at the highest level.

Published rulings, on the other hand, may be relied upon by a taxpayer if the facts and circumstances of his case are substantially the same. Moreover, they will not be changed retroactively.

The IRS' private revenue ruling procedure has been criticized as allowing inconsistency and discouraging reliance on administrative precedent. However, it does permit the agency to expand its interpretative service at a relatively authoritative level without incurring the delay and expense of a more formal process. The difficulty is that such IRS advice is secret. Private rulings should be available for public inspection (though probably unpublished) with the caveat that the Service may deviate from them, even retroactively, for good reason—which may simply be that the prior ruling is considered erroneous. Though the taxpayer would still be aware that any reliance upon a private ruling would be at his peril, the availability of such rulings would encourage consistent decisions. Since only professionals would be aware of the rulings the taxpayer would be properly advised.

Other agencies have similar, yet distinctive systems. At the SEC, issuers are given staff advice in the form of "no action" letters (about 5,-000 annually). These opinions are published. While they are technically not binding on the Commission, as a practical matter the SEC does not deviate retrospectively. The FTC does not authorize its staff to publish its views and has no formal procedures for an interpretative service at the staff level. However, it does issue public advisory opinions (about 200 per year) after review by the Commission, and these opinions are modified prospectively only. (Expert FTC practitioners are also aware that informal opinions will be issued by the staff and that as a practical matter the Commission adheres to them.) In its supervision of labels on hazardous substances, the FDA responds to approximately 650 informal requests each year through nonpublic staff opinions. In most instances, the only question is whether the precautionary label is adequate; however, the staff sometimes uses the occasion to urge the manufacturer to substitute less harmful components for those requiring special labeling.

In addition, almost every administrative agency issues statements of general policy and interpretations of the statutes under which they operate. These serve to guide both the agency staff and the persons they regulate by indicating the agency's views and how it operates. These rulings are not binding upon those affected (although they may be on the agency) and they may be issued without prior formal consultation (through notice and hearing) with affected persons. Section 3 of the APA—the Freedom of Information Act—generally requires that these policy pronouncements be published in the Federal Register. 5 U.S.C.A. § 552.

Several problems frequently arise in connection with informal opinions. First, from the view of the lawyer advising a client, should informal advice be sought? Here no standards or rules can be suggested, but one can note several relevant considerations. Administrators are human, and the lawyer should not test their patience by seeking their advice without some advance preparation. Informal advice is given to fill information gaps, not to train the lawyer about agency procedures. Requesting an opinion also draws the agency's attention to a matter which otherwise might go unnoticed. The agency may take an unfavorable position and then not allow the private party to withdraw the request. It is no coincidence that the FDA staff is not asked for advice on the labeling of products containing banned substances.* In other words,

---

* The FDA staff also reports that "many manufacturers submit requests for advisory opinions on advice of counsel with the chief goal being defensive use of the opinions in the event of liability suits by injured customers." Heffron, Federal Consumer Safety Legislation 179 (Special Report for National Commission on Product Safety 1970). However, where FDA approval of a drug is required before it can be marketed if it is "new" or a "food additive" (not on the GRAS list), informal inquiries are seldom submitted on the apparent assumption that the FDA's response will

obtaining informal advice is not always "cost free."

A second problem involves the reliability of the informal ruling. Viewing the issue from the administrator's side, is the agency estopped if the regulated person relies upon administrative advice which is later found to be erroneous? The regulated party asserts that he has relied upon government advice and that it is unfair for the government to change its position to his detriment. On the other hand, the agency can argue that it should not be bound by the views of low echelon personnel and that reliance was unreasonable in light of its source. Furthermore, to permit estoppel would persuade the government to eliminate its interpretative service; and this would be a detriment to all regulated parties. Other interests may also be at stake. For example, in Wilmington Chemical Corp. v. Celebrezze, 229 F.Supp. 168 (N.D.Ill.1964), a manufacturer of waterproofing basement paint argued that the FDA could not require a more stringent label on paint already marketed since the cans were labeled in reliance on an earlier advisory opinion. The court rejected this contention when the FDA pointed out that it had later learned that a "mere spark"—such as a house furnace

invariably be adverse, obliging the manufacturer then to comply with the preclearance procedure.

starting up—had touched off explosions killing users of the improperly labeled product. It seems that whether estoppel will be applied to informal advice depends on the nature of the reliance, the relative position of the parties, the potential detriment suffered by each, and the impact of estoppel on the administrative operation. Compare Federal Crop Ins. Corp. v. Merrill, 332 U.S. 380, 68 S.Ct. 1 (1947), with Moser v. United States, 341 U.S. 41, 71 S.Ct. 553 (1951).

Finally, there is the question of review. If the agency refuses to render a ruling or its ruling is unfavorable, can the regulated party obtain judicial relief? Section 5(d) of the APA sought to formalize informal advice by authorizing agencies to "issue a declaratory order to determine a controversy or remove uncertainty." 5 U.S.C.A. § 554(e). The advantage of a declaratory order over an informal opinion is its binding effect generally and the availability of review. Nevertheless, neither agencies nor attorneys practicing before them have availed themselves of this procedure very often. Few agency rules specifically refer to a declaratory order procedure, and its limits are untested. This seems surprising in light of the increasing need for reliable guidance and binding rulings. One explanation is that section 5(d) is limited by the introductory exceptions to section 5 to the agency's "sound discretion," and by the requirement that it applies only to matters required to be determined on the record after a hearing. Moreover, agencies rightly shrink from advising individuals how close they can maneuver to the line of illegality without crossing over it—a possible misuse of the declaratory order procedure.

The more difficult question continues to be whether an adverse informal ruling can be reviewed. (It seems clear that a regulated party cannot force an agency to make an informal ruling or to issue a declaratory order; it must seek pre-enforcement review of the rule or await prosecution and challenge the agency's position as part of the defense.) On the one hand, review allows a party to have his rights determined without having to risk administrative or criminal sanctions. No agency proceeding is short-circuited and no regulatory procedure is frustrated. Arguing against review, agencies rightly point out that review is not costless to them. It forces them to use their resources in determining whether to oppose the respondent, then to argue against respondent if necessary, etc. They also raise again the in terrorem argument that permitting review will discourage the practice of giving informal advice, with a resulting loss to all regulated parties. Earlier rulings rejected the possibility of judicial review. International Longshoremen's & Warehousemen's Union v. Boyd, 347 U.S. 222, 74 S.Ct. 447 (1954); Helco Prods. Co. v. McNutt, 137 F. 2d 681 (D.C. Cir. 1943). Recently, courts have substantially broadened the scope of reviewability. See Abbott Laboratories v. Gardner, 387 U.S. 136, 87 S.Ct. 1507 (1967). And in Citizens to Preserve Overton Park, Inc. v. Volpe, 401 U.S. 402, 91 S.Ct. 814 (1971), the Supreme Court held that where federal statutes prohibit the Secretary of Transportation from approving use of public parks for interstate highways unless there is "no feasible and prudent alternative," his decision (made without a prior formal hearing) is subject to judicial review. Although the substantial evidence rule is not applicable, the Court ruled that section 10(e) of the APA requires that the Secretary's action not exceed his delegated authority, abuse his discretion, or fail to comply with procedural requirements. Unless there is a significant threat of substantial harm and subsequent review will be inadequate, however, it seems unlikely that a court will be willing to review an informal ruling.

CHAPTER VII

FORMAL PROCESSES: RULES AND RULEMAKING

Informal administrative action may be unsatisfactory if either the administrator or the regulated party is unwilling to negotiate or accept the other's minimum position. Thorough and impartial procedures are necessary for hearing these cases where the claimant or regulated person and the agency are unable to iron out differences. Nor will an informal ruling guide other parties if they are uninformed about the ruling or their position is substantially dissimilar. In order to advise regulated persons how statutes will be interpreted and applied or to fill in a legislative design, further information may be needed and additional views heard. In such cases, administrative agencies rely upon formal procedures to give notice and a hearing to named and interested parties so that they may present evidence and argument before policies are formulated and applied.

Most formal proceedings fall into one of two categories: rulemaking or adjudication. Rulemaking involves the formulation of a policy or interpretation which the agency will apply in the future to all persons engaged in the regulated activity. Adjudication is the administrative equivalent of a judicial trial. It applies policy to a set of past actions and results in an order against (or in favor of) the named party. The focus of rulemaking is prospective. The primary focus of adjudication is retrospective. However, where formal procedures are relied upon—that is, in either rulemaking or adjudication—the agency will usually give interested or affected persons notice and an opportunity to be heard before the rule or order is issued.

A. RULES

General rules and regulations promulgated by the executive have been a feature of federal and state governments since they were first established. Administrative rules have developed as the field of governmental regulation has expanded and Congress has relied increasingly upon skeletal legislation authorizing the agency to fill in the details. Acting as a quasi-legislative body, agencies issue three types of rules: procedural, interpretative, and legislative.

Procedural rules identify an agency's organization, describe its method of operation, and spell out the requirements of its practice for rulemaking and adjudicative hearings. Although it is not required, regulated persons and interested observers are frequently consulted before procedural rules are written or revised. These house-keeping rules are usually authorized by the agency's enabling act and are binding on the agency. In other words, an agency decision will usually be reversed if a regulated party can show that the agency did not comply with its own rules (even if the agency was not required to adopt these rules). Service v. Dulles, 354 U.S. 363, 77 S.Ct. 1152 (1957).

Interpretative rules are issued by an agency to guide both its staff and regulated parties as to how the agency will interpret its statutory mandate. They range from informally developed policy statements announced through a press release to authoritative rulings binding upon the agency and issued only after interested and affected persons are given notice and an opportunity to be heard. The notice and hearing requirements of the APA need not be followed. As a practical matter, however, where time permits and the regulated or affected persons are likely to have evidence or argument to present, agencies often hold open hearings allowing anyone to comment and submit their views upon the proposed interpretative rule. Since an interpretative rule merely sets forth the administering agency's opinion on the meaning of a statute or its terms (that is, the legislature did not specifically delegate authority to the agency to define or fill in the terms), its interpretation is significant but not necessarily binding on the parties. If challenged in court and upheld, the ruling is binding on the agency and parties until changed prospectively. However, the court is (theoretically) free to substitute its own understanding of the legislative design by inquiring into the "rightness" or propriety of the rule. If the court disagrees with the agency's interpretation, the rule binds neither the agency nor the regulated parties. However, courts are generally reluctant to overturn agency judgments. It is the agency, not the court, which is the legislatively designated expert, and the agency is thought to know what effective regulation needs. Yet if this view were carried to its logical conclusion, judicial review would be a nullity. Consequently, courts are more likely to accept the correctness of interpretative rulings where the administrative competence is substantially superior to the courts. Courts have also recognized interpretative rules when the legislature has had ample opportunity to change them and has failed to do so. Thus, binding effect is given to long-standing interpretative rules and to interpretations adopted before the statute was re-enacted without substantial change. Similarly, interpretative rules issued contemporaneously with the passage of the statute are seldom reversed on the theory that the legislature must have known and approved the agency's interpretation. Upon close examination, it seems clear that these "guides" apply when the court does not substantially disagree with the administrative interpretation. These guides may be conclusory rationalizations rather than neutral principles by which a reviewing court will examine an interpretative rule.

Legislative or substantive rules are, in effect, administrative statutes. In issuing a legislative rule, the administrator exercises lawmaking power delegated to him by the legislature. Notice and a hearing must usually precede issuance of the rule. (Distinctions between interpretative and legislative rules are not always clear because the legislative delegation needed to support a legislative rule is often very vague.) A clear example of a legislative rule and the limits of the administrator's authority to issue a legislative rule is provided in *Addison v. Holly Hill Fruit Products, Inc.,* 322 U.S. 607, 64 S.Ct. 1215 (1944). The Fair Labor Standards Act sets minimum wage requirements in various industries. However, it exempts employees "within the area of production (as defined by the administrator)" engaged in canning agricultural commodities for market. The statute, in other words, authorizes the administrator to determine which canning workers are not covered by the Act because they work within the area where the commodities are grown. (The provision obviously is a concession to farmers who do not want to see their exempt workers enticed by higher paying canning factory jobs and to canning manufacturers who want to keep labor costs down.) In *Holly Hill* the administrator had defined the "area of production" to include, inter alia, canneries employing seven or fewer workers. On review, the Supreme Court held the rule ineffective and ultra vires because in defining the *area* of production the administrator had exceeded his delegated authority by using the *number* of employees in a particular plant as a test of exemption. In other words, legislative rules are binding and a reviewing court will give the rule the force and effect of law only if it is authorized and constitutional.

Whether procedural, interpretative, or legislative, certain characteristics identify administrative rules and distinguish them from other formal administrative actions, particularly orders. The APA defines a rule as "the whole or part of an agency statement of general or particular applicability and future effect designed to implement, interpret, or prescribe law or policy or describing the organization, procedure, or practice requirements of any agency . . . ." 5 U.S.C.A. § 551(4). The most distinguishing feature of a legislative or interpretative rule is that it operates prospectively by stating an administrative judgment about the future, rather than a determination of what happened in the past. (However, an agency's interpretative rule may affect existing conduct in the same manner as an order and may also be relied upon by the agency in applying a statute to prior conduct—unless the new rule contradicts a prior agency rule.) Other frequent attributes of an administrative rule are that it (a) applies generally (usually to a group which may subsequently include new members), (b) results in sanctions against an individual only after a further (adjudicative) proceeding, and (c) involves general (legislative) rather than specific (adjudicative) facts.

B. RULEMAKING

In a broad and rather unilluminating passage, the APA defines rulemaking as any "agency process for formulating, amending, or repealing a rule." 5 U.S.C.A. § 551(5). Section 4 commands that whenever an agency engages in rulemaking, it shall publish an *advance notice* in the Federal Register announcing the proposed rulemaking, afford interested persons an opportunity to *participate* "through submission of written data, views, or arguments with or without opportunity for oral presentation," and *publish* the finally adopted rule "30 days before its effective date." 5 U.S.C.A. § 553(b), (c), (d). The reach of these requirements is limited by a series of exceptions interspersed throughout section 4. Unless required by another statute these minimal standards do not apply when an agency adopts procedural or interpretative rules. In fact, in formulating legislative rules the agency need not give advance notice, an opportunity to participate, or defer the effective date if it finds that there is "good cause" for avoiding these commands.

Consequently, most administrative rules are formulated without advance notice or public hearings. This does not mean that agencies write rules in secret and then spring them as a surprise on affected parties. Where desirable, the usual practice is to consult informally with interested persons (selected by the agency) or advisory committees, or the rule is developed in response to petitions and requests for advice. However, it is true that many rules are routine, do not involve any controversy, and therefore do not warrant formal notice or hearing procedures.

Most rulemaking falls into the "notice-and-comment" category. Section 4 of the APA does not command the holding of a trial-type hearing in any federal rulemaking; it requires only that the proposed rule be announced in advance and that interested parties should be afforded an opportunity to present their views. Even when rule-making procedures are exempt from section 4, agencies often allow an opportunity for formal public participation in framing rules. When an agency invites public participation, it has wide discretion in setting the format of the proceeding. It may limit the "hearing" to written submissions on a private or public record (except section 3 requires that most comments be available to the public upon request) or to oral presentations of factual statements and arguments. The hearing often resembles a legislative hearing—which is appropriate since the agency is acting as a sublegislature. Like legislative committees, the agency is free to consider material not presented in the rulemaking hearing; thus it is not bound by the evidence in the record. This point was explained in Pacific Coast European Conference v. United States, 350 F.2d 197, 205 (9th Cir. 1965): "It is apparent that in rulemaking hearings the purpose is to permit the agency to educate itself and not to allow interested parties to choose the issues or narrow the scope of the proceedings. The purpose of the notice is to allow interested parties to make useful comment and not to allow them to assert their 'rights' to insist that the rule take a particular form. The agency, in rulemaking, can look beyond the particular hearing record since it otherwise would be unable to draw upon its expertise."

An additional, though infrequently used, rulemaking procedure is described as "rulemaking on a record." It is almost indistinguishable from an adjudicative proceeding. This process involves the promulgation of rules (usually legislative) only after a formal evidentiary hearing, including cross-examination and the development of detailed findings of fact and conclusions of law supported entirely on the record developed at the formal hearing. Specific statutory provisions require this procedure for the development of food standards and commodity marketing orders. The process has proved unwieldy and does not result in qualitatively superior rules. For example, it took the FDA over nine years to fix a federal standard for the peanut content of peanut butter. Even then, two manufacturers obtained a stay pending the outcome of their judicial appeal!* It is not surprising that this statutorily imposed procedure has been savagely (and justly) criticized. Whether peanut butter should be 78% (as some manufacturers wanted) or 90% (as the FDA staff and consumers advocated) peanuts is hardly conducive to analysis by trial-

* Another recent FDA hearing to fix staudards for vitamins and mineral additives involved 110 parties; each had the right to present evidence and cross-examine witnesses.

type procedures. Trial procedures are designed to resolve factual disputes; and the "peanut butter parties" were not in disagreement over any fact question, such as the actual peanut content of peanut butter then on the market. Rulemaking usually involves policy issues (i. e., value judgments) which depend upon the agency's being informed about current practices, the impact of the proposed rule, the need for public protection against inadequate safeguards, and the possible burden (cost, freedom, etc.) of government regulation on private interests. In most situations, rulemaking determinations lend themselves to written submissions or oral argument. Where there is a factual dispute or an expert's opinion needs testing, it may be desirable to allow affected parties to treat the rulemaking proceedings as adversary. However, the decision to have a trial-type hearing should be an administrative choice, not an inflexible legislative command.

CHAPTER VIII

FORMAL PROCESSES: ORDERS AND ADJUDICATIONS

Most administrative enforcement relies upon informal methods including advisory letters, administrative warnings, and settlement stipulations. Like their judicial counterparts, however, agencies also rely upon trial-type proceedings for deciding disputed questions of fact, determining policy in a precise factual setting, and ordering compliance with specific laws and regulations.

Although comparative figures are inexact, the conclusion is indisputable that administrative trials far exceed the number of judicial trials. For example, in fiscal 1963 (the most recent figures available) almost 70,000 administrative trials involving oral testimony and verbatim transcripts were heard by the more than 100 agencies of the federal government. In comparison, the federal district courts heard fewer than 11,000 civil and criminal cases that year, and not even 6,000 of these were jury trials. Moreover, the subject matter and significance of administrative trials equal those facing the courts. Administrative trials range from relatively insubstantial individual workmen's compensation claims to precedent setting antitrust merger rulings involving millions of dollars and affecting thousands of employees.

A. ORDERS

Administrative orders are simply the end-product of administrative adjudications. They are usually directed at a named party and may cover license determinations. 5 U.S.C.A. § 551 (6), (7).

B. ADJUDICATIONS

Federal administrative proceedings which culminate in orders usually are governed by the general provisions of the APA codifying traditional judicial practices of apprisal, counsel, confrontation, cross examination and an impartial tribunal. 5 U.S.C.A. §§ 554–57. In addition, each agency conducting adjudicatory hearings has adopted detailed rules of practice (procedural rules) which are initially published in the Federal Register and then collected in the Code of Federal Regulations.

At first glance many, and perhaps most, administrative adjudications appear to be merely carbon copies of judicial trials. The majority are usually open to the public and conducted in an orderly and dignified manner, though not necessarily with the formality of a judicial trial. Typically, the proceeding is initiated by the agency's filing of a complaint in a manner similar to the procedure followed in a civil action. Following the respondent's answer, discovery and pre-hearing conferences may be held. At the trial, an examiner presides by conducting the hearing and ruling on all motions. The agency is repre-sented by counsel who presents evidence in either written or oral question-and-answer form in sup-port of the complaint. The respondent then pre-sents his case in the same fashion. Witnesses may be cross-examined, objections may be raised, and rulings issued. The parties usually submit briefs and proposed findings to the examiner. They may also make oral argument. Shortly after the hearing ends, the examiner renders a decision, usually supported by findings and a written opinion. If neither agency counsel nor respondent objects, the recommended order is customarily adopted by the agency. If there are exceptions, the agency will review the decision in the manner of an appellate court through the submission of briefs and oral argument by both parties. In general, therefore, a lawyer experi-enced in litigating cases in state or federal courts will not find an administrative hearing strange or unfamiliar. The parties are represented by counsel; the examiner is treated with deference; and the evidence is received in the usual ques-tion-and-answer form.

Variations from this general pattern are nei-ther uncommon nor insignificant. Many adjudicatory hearings are conducted informally without the presence of attorneys and by hearing officers without legal training. In some instances, an action may be initiated by a private party rather than by the agency, such as the granting of a license or the approval of a rate request.

Another and more significant distinction between judicial and administrative adjudications is that agency hearings tend to produce evidence of general conditions as distinguished from facts relating solely to the respondent. This difference is attributable to one of the original justifications for administrative agencies—the development of policy. Administrative agencies more consciously formulate policy by adjudicating (as well as by rulemaking) than do courts. Consequently, administrative hearings require that the hearing officer consider the impact of his decision upon the general public interest as well as upon the particular respondent. Testimonial evidence and cross-examination therefore often play less decisive roles in many administrative hearings.

A close examination of administrative adjudication discloses additional significant institutional differences between agency and court trials. Foremost among these distinctions is the fact that an administrative hearing is tried to the *trial examiner* and never to a *jury*. Since many of the rules governing the admission of proof in judicial trials are designed to protect the jury from unreliable and possibly confusing evidence, these rules need not be applied with the same vigor in proceedings solely before a judge or trial examiner. Consequently, the rules of evidence applied in jury trials presided over by a judge are frequently inapplicable in an administrative trial. The trial examiner decides both the facts and the law to be applied. He is usually a lawyer and is often an expert on the very question he must decide.

Another distinction arises from the fact that courts accept whatever cases the parties present. Consequently, their familiarity with the subject matter is accidental. Agencies, on the other hand, usually select (prosecute) their cases. Trial examiners and agency chiefs are either experts or at least have a substantial familiarity with the subject matter since their jurisdictions tend to be restricted. Moreover, an agency usually is staffed by experts whose reports, commonly relating to matters adjudicated before the agency, are made available to examiners and commissioners alike. While this development of agency experience and expertise is often offered as a justification for administrative agencies, it nevertheless creates a basic conflict between assuring fairness to the respondent on the one hand

and promoting efficient use of reliable information on the other. For example, the respondent may want an opportunity to rebut or explain all the "evidence" which the examiner or agency relies upon in making its decision. Yet the agency will want to avoid the burden of having to prove again "facts" which it previously established. As a result agencies have developed the doctrine of "official notice" in administrative hearings. This concept builds upon the doctrine of judicial notice long applied in judicial proceedings. Briefly, the administrative law concept of official notice requires that an agency give the respondent prior notice and an opportunity to rebut any material "trial" facts which the agency would otherwise presume to exist. 5 U.S.C.A. § 556(e).

CHAPTER IX

REQUIREMENTS OF A HEARING AND THE DEVELOPMENT OF POLICY

Our focus now shifts from the form of administrative proceedings to the circumstances in which administrative action must be preceded by notice and a hearing—particularly, by an opportunity to be heard in an adjudicative setting. Several questions arise. Must the agency allow anyone affected by the agency's substantive decision an opportunity to test its basis? What type of hearing is commanded? Are there any exceptions and when and for what?

A. RULEMAKING OR ADJUDICATION

In deciding whether to act by rule or order, the administrator must decide which procedure is suited to the agency's task while meeting the demands of fairness by the persons likely to be affected. On the one hand, the agency is urged to spell out its policies in advance so that regulated persons can guide their conduct accordingly. "Overjudicialization" (i. e., acting only by adjudication) is to be avoided because it is cumbersome and costly. Agencies, in contrast to courts, are given authority to act as quasi-legislatures for a purpose. Broad policy planning should be developed in rulemaking proceedings allowing all interested persons—not just a few named parties—an opportunity to participate. Rulemaking proceedings are designed to explore "policy" or "legislative facts" (i. e., industry practices, economic impact, scientific data, alternative choices, etc.) about which the parties have no special information.

On the other hand, policy decisions often have a significant and immediate impact on regulated persons. If the policy foundation is erroneous or based on a factual misunderstanding, the regulated person may rightfully assert that the rule dispossesses him of "life, liberty or property" without "due process of law." He is entitled to prior notice as a named party, to be apprised of the administrative action proposed, and to test it in a fair hearing. If the "rule" applies only to a few persons, it may appear indistinguishable from a proposed order which is "individual in impact and condemnatory in purpose." The "policy" may turn upon "adjudicative facts" (i. e., the who, what, where, when and how questions) about which named parties are most familiar and which can be tested best in a trial. Further, rulemaking is inappropriate where little is known about possible exceptional circumstances, especially when the exceptions will end up swallowing the substantive rule. The genius of the common law is its inductive methodology of moving to general principles only after testing them on concrete facts.

Before considering the limits and limitations on each approach, it should be noted that rulemaking and adjudicatory procedures are not mutually exclusive. Agencies occasionally modify each by borrowing from the other. Cross-examination may be available in rulemaking; written submissions may be all that is allowed in adjudication. In addition, the underlying substantive policy issues are probably of greater significance in shaping procedure than is generally conceded, at least in the case law. There is an artificiality about attempting to consider these procedural questions in a substantive vacuum. Finally, the question of whether to develop policy through case-by-case adjudication or by translating statutory generalities into specific rules, is a question of degree—substantively and procedurally. Administrative regulations are frequently vague. Adjudication may be a useful vehicle for developing and announcing precise rules.

1. CONSTITUTIONAL LIMITATIONS ON RULEMAKING

The dominant constitutional provision in the development of administrative procedure is the due process clause—that no person may be deprived of life, liberty or property without "due process of law." As we have seen, when a statute prescribes a particular procedure, the administrator must comply with that mandate—or, on review, the action will be reversed as being ultra vires. Even if he complies, however, the administrator's action must also meet the due process standard. (The same implied command applies, of course, when no particular procedure is specified by the legislature.)

The meaning of the constitutional command is not obvious. Due process means that procedure which is "due" in light of the circumstances and interests involved. It does not command judicial process.* Nor does it demand the best possible procedure. Instead, it takes account of what is feasible and practical. On the other hand, since the constitutional requirement sets only the minimum standard of what is fair, it does not excuse the agency from adopting less than the best procedures.

Several issues are involved in considering the constitutional standard. First, as is obvious from

* Minimum procedural requirements in other (e.g., judicial) contexts are not automatically applicable to administrative agency proceedings. But they should be rejected only when distinguishable on significant grounds. Similarly, procedural minima elsewhere may not satisfy due process in administrative procedure.

a reading of the due process clause, it does not apply unless the administrative action affects someone adversely. At what point a person becomes sufficiently inconvenienced to be entitled to adequate notice and to an opportunity for a fair hearing (since that is what due process usually requires) will be discussed (see pp. 162–168, infra). The second question is what constitutes a constitutionally adequate hearing.* This issue is the focus of succeeding sections analyzing what procedural shortcuts or temporary or emergency action can be taken when a trial-type proceeding is otherwise required. Finally, there is the basic problem of whether a trial hearing is required in the first place, or will a rulemaking proceeding suffice. That is our immediate concern.

The constitutional foundation indicating when administrative action must be preceded by a trial-type (adjudicative) hearing and when rule-making is permissible appears in two early cases arising out of property assessments and taxes in the city of Denver. In Londoner v. Denver, 210 U.S. 373, 28 S.Ct. 708 (1908), the Board of Public Works, upon petition of a majority of property owners on a street, authorized local improvements and assessed each property without individual hearings "according to the extent that

* The coordinate question of notice and the particulars of adjudicatory hearings are explored in Chapter X, infra.

each one had been specially benefitted." The complaining property owners were given an opportunity to file written complaints, but they were not allowed to present evidence and argument or to test opposing evidence. This procedure was held constitutionally inadequate because individual facts would determine the amount to be assessed against each property and because there was no provision for an individual property owner to "support his allegations by argument, however brief, and, if need be, by proof, however informal."

The contrast case indicating where adjudicatory procedures are not constitutionally mandated is Bi-Metallic Investment Co. v. State Board of Equalization, 239 U.S. 441, 36 S.Ct. 141 (1915). There the administrative agency had increased the valuation of all taxable property in Denver by 40 percent without giving individual property owners notice and hearing. This procedure was upheld: "Where a rule of conduct applies to more than a few people it is impracticable that every one should have a direct voice in its adoption."

While *Londoner* and *Bi-Metallic* can be distinguished (and explained) because of the number of persons directly affected by the administrative action, that is only an initial guide suggesting whether rulemaking or adjudication is likely to be appropriate. It is not dispositive. Adjudication is usually required if only a few persons are involved; rulemaking is usually permissible if large numbers will be affected. But a false advertising charge against all encyclopedia sellers can be decided only after a trial, no matter how many persons are charged. Alternatively, the designation of the "area of production" under the Fair Labor Standards Act for determining which cannery workers are exempt from the minimum wage laws can be determined in a rulemaking proceeding even though very few—or even no one—is in fact within the class when the rule is announced.

The constitutional distinction between *Londoner* and *Bi-Metallic* is not the number of property owners involved, but rather the focus of the proceeding. A property owner usually has a basic right to an individual hearing before an assessment is imposed because of individual facts suitable for testing in a trial-type hearing. Thus, a hearing was required in *Londoner* since the property owner's assessment depended upon how much he benefitted from the improvement (i. e., the footage of his property adjoining the improved street). On the other hand, where the administrator assesses the property owner on general grounds not related to his peculiar situation, separate individual hearings are not constitutionally required. Thus, in *Bi-Metallic* the increased assessment was based on the community's general revenue needs, not any change in the individual taxpayer's position. Note, individual adjudicatory hearings may be required where a high degree of precision is necessary to make a particular judgment; but where the decision depends upon a general evaluation, rulemaking procedures may be adequate.

2. STATUTORY REQUIREMENT OF A HEARING

Enabling legislation often requires that an agency make a determination on the record after a hearing—that is, after a trial before an impartial tribunal—before it denies a license, imposes a sanction, or revokes a benefit. For example, the Communications Act requires the FCC to hold a "full hearing" before a license application is refused. 47 U.S.C.A. § 309(e). The question which has arisen is not what are the attributes of a hearing,* but rather does the agency have authority to rely upon rulemaking to formulate policy and thereby to limit the consideration of issues in a subsequent trial-type hearing.

---

* The minimum attributes of a fair hearing are often an issue in determining procedural requirements protecting the beneficiaries of government largess. See pp. 166–168, infra.

· The leading case exploring this question is United States v. Storer Broadcasting Co., 351 U.S. 192, 76 S.Ct. 763 (1956). The FCC had issued a notice of proposed rule-making to amend its multiple ownership rules (reducing the number of television outlets "controlled" by one person to five). After the FCC issued the rulemaking notice, but before the rule amendment was adopted, Storer applied for an additional station, even though it already held the maximum allowed by the proposed rule. To protect its position, Storer participated in the rulemaking proceeding by filing a statement opposing the amendment. Nonetheless, the Commission adopted the rule as proposed, and simultaneously dismissed Storer's application as not conforming to the new rule.

Storer then sought judicial reversal of the rule, rather than taking an appeal from the dismissal of its application, as being contrary to the "full hearing" requirement of the statute. The Supreme Court sustained the FCC's rulemaking procedure holding that the Commission did not deny Storer its right to a hearing. The multiple ownership rule was authorized by the Communications Act and was not inconsistent with its mandate. As a valid "legislative" rule the amendment was tantamount to a statutory condition; hence Storer's application was properly dismissed as being contrary to the statute. Storer's right to a hearing was adequately protected by its opportunity to appeal from the rule as well as by the rule's provision for flexibility in implementation (i. e., the rule provided for its waiver when its application was inappropriate).

What the Court approved in *Storer*, then, was the use of agency rulemaking power to decide substantive policy. Storer was not denied a hearing, under this theory, since it could not meet the multiple ownership conditions lawfully attached to license applications. What conditions, if any, should attach to broadcast license applications to avoid overconcentration of television facilities is not peculiarly susceptible to determination in a hearing where the evidence is presented by oral testimony and documentary exhibits and is tested by cross-examination. The soundness of the FCC's policy depends upon economic and social considerations developed by the collection of factual data and by the presentation of policy arguments which, upon evaluation, point in a particular direction. In this situation, rulemaking procedures provide adequate assurance that the agency will be apprised of the information necessary for a sound decision since witness credibility is usually not in issue and the accuracy of each fact determination is relatively insignificant, as long as the data mass is generally accurate.

[*147*]

Nor is the procedure unfair to license applicants. The question of multiple ownership applies to all license applicants who are or might be affected and should be decided only after they have an opportunity to present their views. Rulemaking allows for notice and an opportunity for everyone to be heard before the new rule is adopted. Peculiar circumstances applicable to a particular applicant which are tested best by adjudicatory procedures are accommodated by the rule's waiver provision.

After *Storer*, the authority to foreclose by rulemaking, issues which usually require adjudicatory procedures went largely unexercised by other agencies. And when it was utilized by the FPC, the Court was called upon to reconsider *Storer* in the context of that agency's regulation. FPC v. Texaco, Inc., 377 U.S. 33, 84 S.Ct. 1105 (1964). The FPC had adopted a rule announcing that it would not consider certificate applications by natural gas producers seeking to supply pipelines if their contracts contained price escalation clauses. Two producers who had participated in the rulemaking proceeding subsequently filed applications containing the forbidden provisions. They then appealed from the Commission's summary rejection of their applications as being violative of section 7 of the Natural Gas Act which required that the FPC "shall set" each application "for hearing." Ruling that *Storer* was not confined to communications regulation, the Court held that the hearing requirement did "not preclude the Commission from particularizing statutory standards through the rulemaking process and barring at the threshold those who neither measure up to them nor show reasons why in the public interest the rule should be waived."

Storer and *Texaco* are important in affirming the elementary power of agencies to develop substantive policy through rulemaking procedures. They left unanswered, however, the scope of agency rulemaking authority and the limitations, if any, which constrain its exercise. For example, in both cases the rule only altered prospective rights. Storer held the maximum number of broadcast stations, but no more; the gas producers in *Texaco* were seeking new certificates, not complaining about alteration of existing certificates. This left open the question: Could an agency use its rulemaking power to alter existing rights or privileges?

Several lower court opinions have concluded that an agency may alter existing licenses through rulemaking where the rule is not "individual in impact and condemnatory in purpose" —that is, where fairness does not require adjudicatory procedures. The leading case is American Airlines, Inc. v. CAB, 359 F.2d 624 (D.C. Cir.)

(en banc), cert. denied 385 U.S. 843, 87 S.Ct. 73 (1966). There the court approved the Board's "blocked space" rule which granted all-cargo carriers (airlines) the exclusive right to sell reserved space on their planes at wholesale rates. The effect of the rule was to deny combination carriers, those airlines carrying passengers as well as cargo, the opportunity to sell reserved cargo space, thus carving out this section of the cargo market for their all-cargo competitors. The combination carriers appealed from the Board's denial of their blocked space tariffs (rate requests) as being in effect a modification of their existing route certificates, since prior to the rule's adoption the combination carriers were not foreclosed from offering similar blocked space rates. They relied on a statutory requirement that existing route certificates could be modified only after a full hearing. 49 U.S.C.A. § 1371(g).

Even though it conceded, at least implicitly, that the blocked space rulemaking did in fact modify the combination carrier certificates, nevertheless, the court sustained the Board's procedure. Rulemaking was an appropriate and practical procedure for deciding which class of carriers should provide blocked space service. More importantly, in light of the statutory hearing requirement, the court concluded that the statutory standard does not require a hearing when the

[*150*]

combination carriers could not show a substantial need for a trial-type hearing or any prejudice resulting from the CAB's reliance on rulemaking rather than adjudication. "Nowhere in the record is there any specific proffer by petitioners as to the subjects they believed required oral hearings, [or] what kind of facts they proposed to adduce . . . ." See also Upjohn Co. v. Finch, 422 F.2d 944 (6th Cir. 1970) (burden properly imposed on manufacturer to submit substantial evidence that previously certified drugs are effective and safe); Pfizer v. Richardson, 434 F.2d 536 (2d Cir. 1970).

In other words, statutory hearing requirements do not preclude agency reliance on rulemaking procedures when the substantive policy question lends itself to decision in a rulemaking proceeding and that procedure is not unfair. Or to look at the other side of the question, a trial would seem to be required when the issue is whether the respondent has violated a rule or statute, whether a fine is to be assessed, or whether a license is to be revoked or modified because of particularized conduct.*

---

* On the other hand, three of the eight judges sitting in *American Airlines,* including the then Judge Burger, concluded that an adjudicatory hearing was necessary before existing certificate rights could be lawfully modified.

3.   AGENCY DISCRETION

Similar restrictions do not limit agency use of adjudicatory procedures. As the Supreme Court stated in *Chenery II* (SEC v. Chenery, 332 U.S. 194, 203, 67 S.Ct. 1575, 1580 (1947)), "the choice made between proceeding by general rule or by indvidual, ad hoc litigation is one that lies primarily in the informed discretion of the administrative agency."

On the one hand, rulemaking announcing an agency policy before it is applied seems preferable because: the agency has a greater opportunity to collect data needed for the decision; all persons are treated alike and are advised in advance of the standard they are expected to meet; notice of the policy is transmitted more effectively and those affected can plan their conduct to comply with the announced standard; the agency's job of enforcement should be simpler. On the other hand, adjudicatory procedures better protect other interests: the agency may not have enough facts or experience to formulate general rules (even after notice-and-comment hearings); until it obtains the data or gains experience, some regulation may still be necessary; the agency may be unable to anticipate in advance all activities needing regulation; sound and fair rules may need to be tested first in concrete fact situations or in an adversarial context (however, rulemaking can be adversarial); existing rules may need to be made flexible. Thus, despite frequent calls for agencies to employ rulemaking procedures, the rule of *Chenery II* that agencies have broad discretion in their choice of procedures—and may select to operate through case-by-case adjudication—still stands.

There is some suggestion now, however, that the notice and participation requirements of section 4 of the APA (5 U.S.C.A. § 553) impose an outer limit on agency discretion to rely solely upon adjudicatory procedures. In NLRB v. Wyman-Gordon Co., 394 U.S. 759, 89 S.Ct. 1426 (1969), the Labor Board sought to enforce an order based on its *"Excelsior* Rule." That rule, which required employers to furnish unions with a list of their employees prior to representation elections, arose out of a prior adjudicatory decision. Instead of issuing the rule in a subsequent rulemaking proceeding, the Board sought to apply it to Wyman-Gordon. The Supreme Court, in a plurality opinion, upheld the Board's order. Six justices, however, expressly disapproved of the Board's issuance of the rule in an individual adjudication without complying with section 4 of the APA, even though both employers and unions had participated as invited amici in the prior *Excelsior* proceeding and the "rule" had not been applied to the parties in that litigation.

The Court did not suggest that whenever rule-making is appropriate under *Storer/American Airlines* it is now mandatory under the *Wyman-Gordon* dictum. None of the four opinions, in fact, suggested that *Chenery II* was unsound. Nor was the Court able to specify criteria useful for identifying when a rulemaking proceeding is necessary, or even preferable. The central point —and objectionable feature of the NLRB's practice—was that an individual case should not be singled out to develop and announce general rules seemingly independent of the facts and issues in the particular litigation. If the notice and participation requirements of section 4 of the APA mean anything, administrative policy should not be promulgated by adjudicatory procedures unless they are developed incidentally in the course of deciding the particular case. Even then, rule-making procedures should be held reasonably thereafter unless further experience with the rule seems called for. Where a substantive policy needs to be developed and a choice between rulemaking or adjudication exists, the decision (at least initially) on which procedure to use should turn upon the type of information needed by the agency, the evidence which can be expected from the parties, and the fairness of announc-

[*154*]

ing and applying it to the parties to the litigation.

B. PROCEDURAL SHORTCUTS

Where a trial-type proceeding is required, the constitutional command is, of course, satisfied by an administrative trial which precedes the order. It may also be satisfied by making a hearing available after the order is issued but before it becomes "irrevocably fixed." For example, in Nickey v. Mississippi, 292 U.S. 393, 54 S.Ct. 743 (1934), individual property taxes were assessed without either notice and hearing or provision for review by the assessor or a review board. Nevertheless the procedure withstood constitutional challenge because the tax could only be collected in a civil action which meant, in this instance, de novo review in the judicial hearing. In other words, a subsequent judicial hearing can be substituted for the administrative trial as part of the statutory scheme. See First Nat'l Bank of Smithfield v. Saxon, 352 F.2d 267 (4th Cir. 1965); Jordan v. American Eagle Fire Ins. Co., 169 F.2d 281 (D.C. Cir. 1948).

Similarly, "[t]he demands of due process do not require a hearing, at the initial stage or at any particular point or at more than one point in an administrative proceeding so long as the requisite hearing is held before the final order becomes effective." Opp Cotton Mills v. Administrator, Dep't of Labor, 312 U.S. 126, 152–53, 61 S.Ct. 524, 536 (1941). Several agencies issue provisional orders without a prior hearing, but a hearing is available upon request before the order becomes effective. The provisional order offers a practical advantage to the administrator in that it will become final unless the affected person comes forward and requests a hearing. And most provisional orders are never contested. The taxpayer in *Nickey*, on the other hand, could simply sit back and do nothing since the assessment was not effective until the assessor sued; * in this situation the administrative order is said to be preliminary rather than provisional.

Occasionally, agencies have gone even further in putting the burden of seeking a hearing upon the affected person by providing that a hearing is available only upon a showing that a trial-type hearing is necessary. The wage-price freeze imposed during the Second World War relied upon this approach in setting rent ceilings. The Supreme Court upheld this procedure whereby the administrator first set the maximum rent and then, upon a protest, decided from the written

---

* However, the statute may also provide that de novo judicial review must be sought within a specified time period or the scope of review in the enforcement action will otherwise be limited—in which case the two procedures are less distinct.

evidence whether an oral hearing was required. Bowles v. Willingham, 321 U.S. 503, 64 S.Ct. 641 (1944).

It is still unsettled, however, whether the right to a hearing can be conditioned upon a showing by the person requesting the hearing. That is, is it permissible for an agency to require the affected person to act within a limited time period or waive his right to a hearing? Can the agency put the burden of showing that a fact dispute exists warranting a hearing upon the party seeking a trial? Where the regulated person is a business entity or where emergency economic stabilization is involved, it seems clear that the opportunity for a hearing can be so conditioned. Whether the same results follow where personal dignity or an individual's economic survival is at stake seems less certain today in light of analogous doctrinal developments. Cf. Goldberg v. Kelly, 397 U.S. 254, 90 S.Ct. 1011 (1970); Sniadach v. Family Finance Corp., 395 U.S. 337, 89 S.Ct. 1820 (1969).

When an agency decides to proceed by adjudication or a hearing is required, the appropriate procedure may be something less than a judicial style trial. First, a hearing to take evidence is wasteful and usually unnecessary if the facts are not in dispute. Summary judgment, demurrers, etc. may be relied upon in administrative as well as judicial hearings when an evidentiary hearing would serve no useful purpose. See, e. g., Citizens for Allegan County, Inc. v. FPC, 414 F.2d 1125 (D.C. Cir. 1969). Such devices, in fact, honor the right to be heard by allowing the party opposing the motion to show the necessity for a hearing and by placing the burden on the party seeking to avoid a trial. Fairness is protected by relieving the parties of the burdens of a trial in those instances where it is reasonably clear that the ultimate decision can be based upon evidence which can be presented without oral testimony.

Similarly, agencies can limit the hearing to written presentations where credibility is not in issue. Shortened trial procedures limiting oral testimony are used most successfully in rate or price control proceedings, where economic and expert analysis rather than sensorily perceived phenomena provide the bulk of the evidence. It is also becoming clear that agencies can experiment with other approaches such as legislative type hearings (i. e., the information being supplied by oral and written argument), a conference approach (i. e., discussion by the parties with sworn testimony where needed) and other devices shortening the hearing and dispensing with some of the attributes of a judicial trial. See, e. g., Marine Space Enclosures, Inc. v. FMC,

420 F.2d 577, 587–90 (D.C. Cir. 1969) (dicta approving use of briefs, oral argument and affidavits); Moore-McCormack Lines, Inc. v. United States, 413 F.2d 568, 590 (Ct.Cl.1969) ("This is an instance, we believe, in which the need, at the administrative level, is not for a formal trial but for better 'opportunity for party participation in the determination of the governmental action', for 'consultation or conferences, not big open hearings', and for 'a detailed statement of what is contemplated, with an invitation for written comments or data.' "). The disheartening fact, however, is that agency experimentation seldom occurs. Continuing pressures for speedier, yet reliable, hearings suggest that administrative agencies will be forced to experiment with procedural shortcuts with increasing frequency.

C. TEMPORARY ACTION

It is not always possible for agency action to await the deliberate speed of most administrative adjudications. If the administrator were unable to act before the completion of a hearing and subsequent judicial review, his decision may become ineffective and irrelevant because the problem was mooted by intervening events. For example, food and banking regulation depend on swift action; they could be frustrated if contaminated food were not recalled immediately or reckless bank management replaced before the public could react.

At times the need for administrative speed is more significant than the assurance of accuracy and fairness supplied by the adjudicatory hearing. Individual property (and, sometimes, personal) rights must yield temporarily to a compelling public interest in health, safety and security. Where possible, however, evidence must be preserved and a full hearing held as soon as possible, but practical accommodations to public needs often control. . Thus, courts have approved seizure and destruction of contaminated food and drugs even though the owner's right to a full hearing may be impaired, suspension of occupational licenses despite the lack of any provision for reimbursement if the license is reinstated, and interim utility rate reductions or suspension of trading in a security at an unmeasured cost to affected persons. Little attention has been paid toward minimizing the harm resulting from the interim action. Analysis has focused instead on the more basic question of whether the administrative action must be preceded by a hearing.

That the governmental interest in immediate action is not without limit, even when the administrative action is only temporary, is illustrated by Goldberg v. Kelly, 397 U.S. 254, 90 S.Ct. 1011 (1970). The administrator of aid to families with dependent children argued that ineligible recipients could be terminated before any hearing was held to decide eligibility in order that the public treasury could be protected against unlawful payments. The welfare recipient was adequately protected, he said, by subsequent reimbursement if eligibility were re-established, whereas the government was not likely to recoup unlawful payments. The Court rejected this argument. Public assistance benefits are statutory entitlements and therefore protected by procedural due process. Consequently,

> termination of aid pending resolution of a controversy over eligibility may deprive an *eligible* recipient of the very means by which to live while he waits. Since he lacks independent resources, his situation becomes immediately desperate. His need to concentrate upon finding the means for daily subsistence, in turn, adversely affects his ability to seek redress from the welfare bureaucracy. (Id. at 264, 90 S.Ct. at 1018–19.)

The validity of summary administrative action turns on the importance of the public interest in immediate action as compared to the significance of the private right which is to yield on an interim basis. Since many of the leading cases upholding summary action were decided before the Court undertook to require "due process hearings" in areas formerly regarded as mere privileges, the continued validity and permissible scope of summary action is currently undergoing reexamination. Among the questions being tested in the federal courts are whether a hearing must precede termination of a public housing tenancy, of medicare and medicaid benefits, of unemployment compensation and of disability benefits. Other cases have challenged the imposition of prison discipline without a prior hearing, the suspension of a driver's license under financial responsibility laws, and the prehearing repossession of goods with governmental sanction. E. g., compare Bell v. Burson, 402 U.S. 535, 91 S.Ct. 1586 (1971), with Jennings v. Mahoney, 404 U.S. 25, 92 S.Ct. 180 (1971). In each case, the balance must involve not only a careful scrutiny of the administrative action and its justification, but also a consideration of available alternatives. The exercise of summary administrative power is the exception.

D.   THE RIGHT–PRIVILEGE DISTINCTION

The requirement that a welfare recipient be given an opportunity for a pretermination hearing illustrates another aspect of the notice and hearing dilemma. It is universally acknowledged that an opportunity for an adjudicative hearing usually must precede the invocation of administrative authority against the individual. A sanction cannot be imposed, a license cannot be revoked, or an existing certificate cannot be modified unless, in any of these situations, the regulated person is allowed a hearing. One who has a sufficient interest at stake in administrative action is ordinarily entitled to show why he should not be disadvantaged by it.

But frequently the individual interest is asserted to be a mere "privilege." The government is not obliged to provide welfare benefits to the destitute, to build housing for those without adequate shelter, or to create public employment to serve community needs. These statutory entitlements are privileges in the sense that the government is not constitutionally required to provide the benefit and it need not be accepted by the recipient. As a consequence, courts have often applied a "gift" analysis and concluded that the recipient of government largess accepts it on the government's terms—and the government is not barred from imposing any conditions on its grant. As Justice Holmes trenchantly observed, in upholding the summary dismissal of a policeman for political activity: "The petitioner may have a constitutional right to talk politics, but he has no constitutional right to be a policeman." McAuliffe v. Mayor of New Bedford, 155 Mass. 216, 220, 29 N.E. 517 (1892).

On the other hand, such epigrams do not answer whether policemen have any constitutional rights. It is unseemly—and now constitutionally unfair and prohibited—for the government to do indirectly what it cannot do directly. Since the government cannot force a witness to incriminate himself, the Supreme Court has ruled, neither can it condition a private attorney's license to practice law nor a policeman's job on the waiver of the privilege against self-incrimination. Garrity v. New Jersey, 385 U.S. 493, 87 S.Ct. 616 (1967); Spevack v. Klein, 385 U.S. 511, 87 S.Ct. 625 (1967). Just as the government cannot directly discriminate because of race or religion, it cannot condition its largess on unconstitutional criteria.

This doctrine, known as the doctrine of "unconstitutional conditions," assumes that no one has a right to be a policeman. It emphasizes, instead, the rights which a policeman is conceded to possess by explicit provision in the Constitution. The doctrine has been applied, for example, to protect a welfare recipient from being coerced into consenting to a warrantless search of his home absent circumstances otherwise justifying an administrative search. Compare Parrish v. Civil Service Comm'n, 66 Cal.2d 260, 425 P.2d 223, 57 Cal.Rptr. 623 (Sup.Ct.1967), with Camara v. Municipal Court, 387 U.S. 523, 87 S.Ct.

1727 (1967). But see Wyman v. James, 400 U.
S. 309, 91 S.Ct. 381 (1971) (AFDC properly conditioned on consent to welfare caseworker's entry
into recipient's home). Despite the significance
of the protections afforded by the doctrine of
unconstitutional conditions, its reach is limited;
it applies only where the challenged conditions
directly abridge an *explicit* constitutional right.

This has, in turn, led to the doctrinal development that statutory entitlements and other government benefits are now fully protected against
unconstitutional government infringement. Government employees, for example, can no longer
be dismissed for membership per se in political
or economic organizations. Being a member of
the Communist Party or of a labor union is not
a basis for dismissal. Nor can government employment be conditioned on taking an oath for-
swearing activities which a private citizen is constitutionally entitled to pursue. Government largess, in other words, is protected not only by explicit constitutional requirements but also by
the equal protection and due process provisions.
Thus, standards for testing a teacher's competence must be fair and rationally related to his
performance as a teacher (substantive due process), and he must be allowed a fair opportunity
to challenge their application to him (procedural
due process).

Once it is determined that the recipient of government largess has a constitutionally protected right, the question becomes to what degree is that right protected by the Constitution, for "[t]he very nature of due process negates any concept of inflexible procedures universally applicable to every imaginable situation." Cafeteria and Restaurant Workers v. McElroy, 367 U.S. 886, 895, 81 S.Ct. 1743, 1748 (1961). In determining what procedure due process mandates, the precise nature of the governmental function involved is balanced against the private interest affected by governmental action.

The basic standard, for notice and an opportunity to be heard, is set forth in Greene v. McElroy, 360 U.S. 474, 496–97, 79 S.Ct. 1400, 1413 (1959):

> [W]here governmental action seriously injures an individual, and the reasonableness of the action depends on fact findings, the evidence used to prove the Government's case must be disclosed to the individual so that he has an opportunity to show that it is untrue.

Thus, in the case of government employees and teachers, several requirements have been developed which must be satisfied for a constitutional termination of employment.* First, an opportunity for a hearing generally must precede the actual termination. The cost of opposing the dismissal, the injury to reputation from dismissal (even if later reversed), and the limited state interest in immediate termination support the requirement of a pretermination hearing. Where the circumstances warrant, such as when a teacher is charged with conduct endangering his students' welfare, a lesser temporary sanction, such as suspension, may be appropriate pending the hearing. Second, the employee must be given a written statement of reasons for the proposed termination or nonretention, at least if he requests it. Without the notice he is unable to collect evidence and meet the charges. Third, the government employer must provide notice of a hearing at which time the employee may respond. Without advance notice the challenged employee is at an unfair disadvantage. Fourth, and not least, the employee is entitled to a hearing with an opportunity to submit any evidence he might have relative to the stated reasons for termination.

* These requirements are not always or evenly applied, however. For example, in the majority of federal employee removals (outside the post office), the first—and often only—hearing occurs *after*, not before, removal becomes effective.

A host of unanswered questions surrounding the rights of government employees (and of recipients of government benefits) remain to be considered. Must the state provide counsel (as in criminal cases), discovery, a transcript, reasons accompanying the decision, etc.? Do these rights extend to nontenured or probationary employees? About all one can safely predict is that this area of administrative law will be tested frequently in the courts in the years ahead.

CHAPTER X
THE HEARING PROCESS

The variety of administrative adjudicatory procedures cannot be overstressed. Administrative trials range from informal conferences where the presiding officer confers with the parties and witnesses to formal trials applying rigid procedural forms and technical common law rules of evidence, with many intermediate steps in between. It is difficult to suggest how a typical agency operates beyond the general framework outlined earlier (see pp. 133–136, supra). What this discussion seeks, therefore, is to identify distinct problems faced in administrative hearings and to describe how the adjudicatory process deviates from the standard judicial model.

A. PARTIES

1. NOTICE

Persons whose life, liberty or property are the immediate subject of agency action are obviously entitled to notice of the proceedings. Service of notice (i. e., the complaint) is usually accomplished by mail.* Taking a cue from the Federal Rules of Civil Procedure, the general rule is that

---

* Oddly, one of the few exceptions is the Postal Service's rules for fraud order proceedings which provide that personal service is the preferred method. 39 C.F.R. § 952.8 (Postal Service 1971).

"[t]he most important characteristic of pleadings in the administrative process is their unim-
portance." 1 K. C. Davis, Administrative Law
Treatise § 8.04, at 523 (1958). The concept of
"notice pleadings" holds sway. Actual notice
fairly indicating what issues and facts the respondent is to meet and allowing an adequate opportunity to cure surprise is sufficient. Consequently, proof may vary from the pleadings and
pleadings may be amended to conform to proof.

Administrative action frequently has a significant collateral impact. Determination of an
airline's route certificate affects not only the airline, but also its employees, suppliers, customers,
cities along the route, competitors, etc. While
similar problems occur in civil litigation, the
problem of indirect effect is more significant in
many administrative hearings because of their
regulatory scope; agency hearings are not merely private quarrels. The question inevitably
arises: Are those collaterally affected entitled
to notice and to participate in the hearings (and
as parties or nonparties)?

It seems clear that an administrative agency
is not constitutionally required to give notice and
a hearing except to those directly affected—that
is, to named parties—by the administrative action; the administrative order is ineffective as
to persons not made parties to the proceeding.

Administrative agencies must satisfy more than minimal constitutional commands, however. Statutes often require that agencies notify competitors, the public served by regulated parties, "interested persons," etc., of proposed hearings. Federal agencies usually rely upon publication of their notices in the Federal Register to satisfy these commands. By statute the Federal Register is adequate notice unless "insufficient in law." In another context (civil litigation), the Supreme Court has ruled that notice by publication is adequate only "where it is not reasonably possible or practicable to give more adequate warning." Mullane v. Central Hanover Bank & Trust Co., 339 U.S. 306, 317, 70 S.Ct. 652, 658 (1950). *Mullane* suggests, in other words, that published notice may not be sufficient, but the issue is generally untested.

An agency's obligation to provide effective notice also rests on other grounds. To the extent those collaterally affected have relevant information, providing notice and enabling these members of the public to participate contributes to the quality of the agency decision. Hence agencies are giving increasing attention to techniques for providing the public with effective notice of proceedings having a significant impact on them. For example, the AEC now relies upon public service announcements on radio and television, issues press releases, and sends direct invitations to environmental groups in order to notify the affected public about hearings deciding whether to issue atomic power plant construction permits. The FCC requires licensees to make frequent announcement that their licenses are up for renewal and that interested persons can request a hearing and participate. These steps are only the beginning. The focus today is on (a) developing convenient, identified, and accessible sources of information about agency proceedings so that those affected by the decision will have an opportunity to participate; and (b) attracting public attention to significant proceedings since the volume of administrative proceedings is so substantial that, unless sophisticated methods are employed, the practical effect of improved notice procedures may be to decrease the actual notice provided.

2. INTERVENTION

Notifying those who are likely to be affected, even though indirectly, by an agency decision is meaningless unless they may participate in the agency proceedings. The range of possible participation varies from supplying information as witnesses at the call of one of the named parties to intervention as formal parties. The submission of amicus curiae briefs presenting arguments of law and policy is an intermediate alternative. Participation as parties—that is, "standing" to intervene—was, until recently, generally limited to those who could demonstrate that they had a substantial legal interest in, or that they would be "aggrieved" by, the outcome.

But in response to increasing pressure from public interest groups claiming that governmental agencies are unresponsive to public needs and interests, courts have increasingly ruled that interested persons must be allowed an unrestricted opportunity to be heard—and to participate as formal parties—even though they do not have a significant private (i. e., personal or economic) stake in the outcome. (This development followed and now parallels the expansion of standing to seek judicial review discussed at pp. 248–255, infra.)

The first major breakthrough supporting intervention came in Scenic Hudson Preservation Conference v. FPC, 354 F.2d 608 (2d Cir. 1965), where the Second Circuit upset the FPC's rejection of evidence of alternative power sources proffered by conservation groups and others opposing a power plant project. Although the specific holding was limited to a ruling that the statutory standard of "aggrieved person" for purposes of judicial review was satisfied by the aesthetic, conservation and recreation interests

of the petitioners, the court also endorsed the
"private attorney general" concept as justifying
intervention by those without a direct personal
or economic interest in the agency decision.
However, the decision stopped short of conclud-
ing that standing to seek review implied an un-
qualified right to participate fully in the administrative hearing.   Moreover, the opinion left
open the possibility that the FPC's obligation to
receive and consider evidence proffered by public interest groups arose from the FPC's statutory mandate to undertake comprehensive planning as part of its licensing responsibility, and
the case could therefore be distinguished on that
ground.

The next step, and a significant doctrinal advance, came in Office of Communication of the
United Church of Christ v. FCC, 359 F.2d 994
(D.C. Cir. 1966), where the then Judge Burger
held that the listening public's interest in programming content was sufficient to confer
"standing" to intervene in FCC licensing proceedings as well as to seek judicial review.   Once
again the court relied heavily on the private attorney general concept, and on the recognition
that in practice the agency could not always effectively represent the listener interest.   Finally,
while the opinion explicitly left open an area of
agency discretion to structure and limit public

participation by administrative regulation, it also gave short shrift to the FCC's contention that existing avenues of public input, such as the Commission's willingness to hear citizen complaints and have complainants appear as witnesses, were sufficient. Instead, the court simply turned the argument around, and replied that it would be no great burden for the Commission to go a little further and permit the complainants to become formal parties.

Upon review of the remanded decision, the D. C. Circuit again reversed the FCC, this time because the interveners had been forced to assume the burden of proof and had otherwise been treated as "interlopers." 425 F.2d 543 (D.C. Cir. 1969) (Burger, J.). In the course of its opinion, the court made clear that it was adopting the *Scenic Hudson* concept that the agency had an affirmative duty to build a record on the issues raised by the interveners, notwithstanding the absence of any "planning" responsibility in relevant portions of the FCC's organic statute.

Agencies have been slow to respond to these developments, although interveners are now receiving a more hospitable reception.

3. CONSOLIDATION

The proper scope of an adjudicatory hearing and the determination of which parties must be included—the question of consolidation—occurs with increasing frequency as administrative agencies expand the scope of their licensing power and increase the size and number of grants and business they distribute. The issue of consolidation attaches whenever a choice must be made between competing applicants.

The comparative hearing requirement, known as the Ashbacker doctrine, was first developed because the Communications Act provides, as we noted in discussing *Storer* (see p. 145, supra), that before a broadcast license is denied the applicant is entitled to a hearing. In Ashbacker Radio Corp. v. FCC, 326 U.S. 327, 66 S.Ct. 148 (1945), the FCC had before it two applications for licenses to serve different but nearby communities. The applications were mutually exclusive because if both were granted each would create an intolerable electrical interference with the other. The FCC granted one of the licenses without a hearing (the statute required a hearing only if an application was denied) and set the other down for hearing. But it was obvious that the hearing would be a sham because the question to be decided—whether a license should be issued to the applicant—had been precluded by the license previously granted. Consequently, the Supreme Court rendered the common sense judgment that the "full hearing" requirement had not been satisfied; when mutually exclusive applications are filed the agency must consolidate the applications and hear them simultaneously.

Although *Ashbacker* itself involved applications for two separate stations (operating at different frequencies), the doctrine is applied most frequently to require comparative hearings before the FCC and CAB. That is, when two or more persons apply for one broadcast frequency or seek a certificate for a route which can support only one airline, the agency must consolidate the applications. Although the principle is relatively simple to state, it is correspondingly difficult to determine at what point the doctrine applies or when applications are no longer mutually exclusive. The question obviously is one of degree and agencies have considerable discretion. Comparative hearing procedures also involve a question of timing. That is, at what point in time may an agency cut off applications from consideration under comparative hearing requirements. Here each agency's rules are instructive.

B.   EVIDENCE

1.   ADMISSIBILITY

Administrative agencies generally are not restricted in the kind of evidence they can admit.

The APA confirms this practice in section 7(c) by providing that "[a]ny oral or documentary evidence may be received, but the agency as a matter of policy shall provide for the exclusion of irrelevant, immaterial, or unduly repetitious evidence." 5 U.S.C.A. § 556(d). Note, the APA opens the door to *any* evidence which the examiner admits and only *suggests* that insignificant and redundant evidence should be rejected, giving the agencies broad discretion. Moreover, the APA pointedly omits hearsay or other "incompetent" evidence from the list of evidence which should not be received. Thus the exclusion of otherwise legally inadmissible evidence from an administrative hearing may be error. Of course, the exclusion of relevant, material, and competent evidence by a trial examiner will be grounds for reversal if that refusal is prejudicial.

The courts have pressed the agencies to abide by the spirit of these rules. The leading example of such pressure, although decided before the APA was adopted, is found in Samuel H. Moss, Inc. v. FTC, 148 F.2d 378, 380 (2d Cir. 1945), where a distinguished panel of the Second Circuit admonished a hearing examiner for rigidly following the rules of evidence:

> [I]f the case was to be tried with strictness, the examiner was right . . . . Why

either he or the [Federal Trade] Commission's attorney should have thought it desirable to be so formal about the admission of evidence, we cannot understand. Even in criminal trials to a jury it is better, nine times out of ten, to admit, than to exclude, evidence and in such proceedings as these the only conceivable interest that can suffer by admitting any evidence is the time lost, which is seldom as much as that inevitably lost by idle bickering about irrelevancy or incompetence. In the case at bar it chances that no injustice was done, but we take this occasion to point out the danger always involved in conducting such a proceeding in such a spirit, and the absence of any advantage in depriving either the Commission or ourselves of *all evidence which can conceivably throw any light upon the controversy.* (Emphasis added.)

Many reasons support the admission of hearsay and other legally incompetent evidence in administrative hearings. Foremost among them is the fact that these exclusionary rules do not determine the probative value of the proffered evidence. To require that a trial examiner refuse to admit hearsay makes no sense where there is no jury to protect and the trier of fact is equally exposed to the evidence whether he admits or excludes it. Admission without a ruling—as long as the evidence has some element of reliability—does no harm and can prove more efficient than the requiring of a ruling which may later be held erroneous. Discarding the exclusionary rules eliminates the need for the parties to interpose protective objections—the objections being preserved by their briefs to the examiner or agency—and relieves the examiner of making difficult rulings before all the evidence is available. It assures a complete, yet not necessarily unduly long, record and might well avoid the need to reopen the hearing. Hearsay, of course, is not subject to current, in-court cross-examination, but that limitation affects the weight such evidence carries, not its admissibility.

The fact that administrative hearings need not follow the exclusionary rules and the fact that the admission of remote or repetitious evidence is not reversible error do not suggest that "anything goes" or that all proffered evidence, whatever its relevance or trustworthiness, should be admitted. In general, the admissibility of evidence in administrative hearings depends upon the *importance* of the evidence in relation to the ultimate issues rather than to the legal standards of relevance and materiality.

Several significant and useful deviations from the judicial pattern appear in administrative hearings. The first, of course, involves the relatively free receipt of hearsay evidence which appears reliable. Equally important is the manner in which oral testimony is received. Witnesses in agency hearings are frequently permitted to testify in a simple, natural, and direct fashion, without unnecessary interruptions from either the attorney who is directing the questioning or his adversary. A third departure permitted from judicial practice occurs when the examiner is uncertain whether to exclude the evidence on the grounds of incompetency, irrelevancy, or immateriality. In administrative hearings the tendency is to admit the evidence since the need for a complete record and the desirability of avoiding reversal outweigh the disadvantages of a slightly longer record and the delay involved in receiving the evidence.

The more closely administrative proceedings approach judicial proceedings in formality and in the nature of the issues to be tried, the greater the degree to which the exclusionary rules will be applied. Nor has improvement been made to the standard suggested by the Attorney General's Committee on Administrative Procedure in 1941: "The ultimate test of admissibility must be whether the proffered evidence is reliable, probative and relevant. The question in each case must be whether the probability of error justifies the burden of stricter methods of proof."

2. EVALUATION

In contrast to the effect of a trial court's decision to receive hearsay evidence in a jury trial, a hearing officer's decision to receive such evidence in an administrative adjudication is only the first step in determining its impact upon the tribunal's decision. The admission of evidence in a jury trial is often considered the last effective legal control because of the assumption that the jury will rely upon or be swayed by such evidence regardless of whether or not its reliability has been established. In an administrative hearing, on the other hand, as in the case of nonjury trials, it is assumed that the trial examiner will not rely upon untrustworthy evidence in reaching his decision. Thus if there is "competent" or trustworthy evidence to support the decision, the reviewing court presumes that the examiner or trial judge relied on that evidence—and not the "tainted" hearsay—in reaching his decision.

Nevertheless, the more difficult—and often crucial—question for the hearing officer is the determination of whether he should rely upon hearsay evidence in reaching his decision. The examiner's concern is with the reliability or probative worth of the evidence. Jury trial rules of evidence exclude hearsay on the theory that it is untrustworthy unless within an exception. The party against whom the evidence is admitted can neither confront nor cross-examine its original proponent to test its probative worth. But on the other side of the ledger is the fact that each of us constantly relies upon hearsay evidence in making important decisions. Without hearsay, commerce would stop, government would cease to function, and education would be reduced to each teacher's personal experience (and even the latter would often be based on hearsay).

On the other hand, the fact that some hearsay may prove reliable is no guarantee that all hearsay is reliable. Nor is it responsive to observe that the rules of evidence already admit much that is worthless. Why, it could be asked, should more that is worthless be admitted in order to find some that is trustworthy, particularly when there is no assurance that the factfinder will rely on the latter and disregard the former? It could also be contended that unless probative evidence could be distilled or some alternative protection devised, the admission of hearsay would not promote justice. Judge Learned Hand has offered the classic formulation in NLRB v. Remington Rand, 94 F.2d 862, 873 (2d Cir.), cert. denied, 304 U.S. 576, 58 S.Ct. 1046 (1938), rev'd on other grounds, 110 F.2d 148 (2d Cir. 1940) (emphasis added):

> [The examiner] did indeed admit much that would have been excluded at common law, but the act specifically so provides . . . [N]o doubt, that does not mean that mere rumor will serve to "support" a finding, but hearsay may do so, at least if more is not conveniently available, and if in the end the finding is supported by the *kind of evidence on which responsible persons are accustomed to rely in serious affairs.*

Hearing officers and agencies have adhered to this common sense standard instinctively. At the same time, several criteria applied in evaluating the reliability of hearsay can be discerned. The following are the most significant:

(a) What is the "nature" of the hearsay evidence? If the hearsay is likely to be reliable, it usually becomes an exception to the hearsay rule. Moreover, if the evidence is intrinsically trustworthy, agencies have taken the next logical step and relied, if necessary, upon this evidence in deciding cases, even though it technically constitutes hearsay and does not fall within any of the recognized exceptions. An example of hearsay satisfying the reliability criteria is newspaper reports. Stories of significant news events are likely to be reliable, and newspapers normally do not report accidents which did not occur. On the other hand, newspaper summaries of public comments are commonly inaccurate—at least if one may believe those who claim to be misquoted—because of the difficulty of hearing and then summarizing another's views. Even so-called verbatim transcripts commonly suffer from significant errors as a result of the pressure of time deadlines. Note that the hearsay quality of each report is identical. Yet the accident report will be treated as solid support for an administrative decision and the speech summary, unless corroborated, will not. See Montana Power Co. v. FPC, 185 F.2d 491, 498 (D.C.Cir. 1950), cert. denied, 340 U.S. 947, 71 S.Ct. 532 (1951).

(b) Is better evidence available? The necessary substantiation for the reliability of hearsay evidence may arise from the failure of respondent to controvert the hearsay when the proof is readily available to him, even though there is no testimonial or documentary evidence of such available "support." The leading example of this position is United States ex rel. Vajtauer v. Commissioner, 273 U.S. 103, 47 S.Ct. 302 (1927), where the Supreme Court upheld a deportation order based on a finding that the alien had advocated the overthrow of the government by force. The alien gave his name as Emanuel Vajtauer, a "Doctor of Psychology" and editor of the "Spravedlvost." In making his finding the director relied upon two items of hearsay: a pamphlet bearing the name of Dr. E. M. Vajtauer as author; and a newspaper report of a speech by a Dr. Vajtauer, editor of the "Spravedlvost," supporting revolution. Both items became convincing evidence when "the appellant, confronted by this record, stood mute. . . . His silence without explanation other than that he would not testify until the entire evidence was presented, was in itself evidence that he was the author." Workmen's compensation cases furnish a further illustration. In one typical case, the testimony revealed that the workman went home, told his wife that he had been injured while at work, repeated the same story to a doctor, and died. No one saw the accident; no better evidence was available. Placing special reliance on the statute's remedial purpose, the agency relied upon this hearsay evidence even though it fell outside the spontaneous exclamation exception. On the other hand, if credible first-hand witnesses had told another story—for example, that the accident happened elsewhere—the hearing officer would likely have rejected the hearsay testimony, especially if the witnesses' testimony was corroborated by convincing circumstantial evidence. See generally Jacobowitz v. United States, 424 F.2d 555 (Ct.Cl.1970).

(c) How important is the subject matter in relation to the cost of acquiring "better" evidence? Many examples are available. If the out-of-hearing declarant is readily available and the question involves the respondent's livelihood or security—as is often the case in loyalty and deportation matters—hearsay by itself carries little weight. If, however, the matter is but one of thousands of compensation claims—as in social security and workmen's compensation cases—and the declarant's appearance would be relatively costly or time-consuming, hearsay alternatives such as letters or other written evidence might prove decisive. Thus, in Richardson v. Perales, 402 U.S. 389, 91 S.Ct. 1420 (1971), physician's reports adduced by the agency were admissible and satisfied the requirement of "substantial evidence," though opposed by live expert testimony on behalf of the claimant. Considerable emphasis was placed on claimant's failure to subpoena the authors of the reports, although entitled to do so. It has likewise been held that, in the granting of a license, an agency may rely upon evidence which would not be adequate in revoking the same license.

(d) How precise does the agency's factfinding need to be? The ICC's reliance on "typical evidence" and the FTC's use of survey evidence are examples of agency dependence on statistical averages to determine facts in particular cases where legal or policy decisions are not dependent upon exact determinations. For instance, survey evidence indicating that from 9 to 100 percent of the public were misled by respondent's advertising will support a finding that it constitutes an unfair or deceptive act. Still another example is the fixing of a rate for commodities transported by one carrier on the basis of costs incurred by similarly situated carriers.

(e) What is the administrative policy behind the statute being enforced? The range of necessary reliability is affected by the type of policy which the administrative hearing is designed to promote. For example, the social security and workmen's compensation programs are intended to provide benefits quickly at low cost. The refusal to rely upon affidavit facts in such hearings would run counter to the purposes for which the statutes are designed.

When focusing on these criteria, it is essential to consider the central point that evaluation of hearsay and other technically incompetent evidence cannot be accomplished in the abstract; the evidence must be examined in the light of the particular record. This includes, at a minimum, an examination of the quality and quantity of the evidence on each side, as well as the circumstantial setting of the case.

3. SUBSTANTIAL EVIDENCE

Once the agency has determined that legally incompetent evidence can be admitted and relied upon in making an administrative decision, it might appear that the subject of hearsay evidence in administrative hearings has been exhausted. While the agency's admission and use of legally incompetent evidence is subject to judicial review, this review of administrative determinations of fact should be confined to determining whether the decision is supported by the evidence in the record. Judicial review of administrative evidence has not been so limited, however. As a substitute for rules of admissibility, courts apply the so-called "substantial evidence" rule to judicial review of agency action in seeking to assure fairness to the parties.

As applied to administrative findings, the substantial evidence rule possesses two branches, one of which is sound, and the other unsound. The first consists of an overall standard of review of the findings of fact. In essence, it does not differ materially from the "sufficiency" standard applied in judicial review of jury verdicts. It will be examined when we consider the scope of judicial review (see pp. 265–269, infra).

In reviewing administrative decisions, some appellate courts—primarily state—have added a second branch to the substantial evidence test,

[*189*]

warping the test into a rigid rule for denying
credibility to uncorroborated hearsay evidence.
Known as the "legal residuum rule" because it
requires that an administrative finding of fact
be supported by some evidence admissible in a
jury trial—that is, by a residuum of legal evidence—it has been severely criticized, and its application has strained judicial reasoning.

The earliest case applying this rule illustrates
its weakness. In Carroll v. Knickerbocker Ice
Co., 218 N.Y. 435, 113 N.E. 507 (1916), the New
York Court of Appeals reversed a workmen's
compensation award in a death case where the
commission's finding of accidental injury was
based wholly on hearsay testimony of statements
by the deceased workman. The workman, who
developed delirium tremens and died within six
days, had told his wife, a neighbor, and his family
and hospital physicians that a 300-pound cake of
ice had fallen upon his abdomen. Each party related this story to the commission. However,
the case record also contained substantial contradictory evidence. The workman's helper on
the ice truck, along with two cooks working in
the saloon where the ice was delivered, testified
that they were present at the time and place
where the accident presumably occurred but they
neither saw nor heard the incident. In addition,
the hospital physicians found no bruises, discol-

orations, or abrasions on the workman's body. In light of the lack of testimonial or physical corroboration of the workman's story which probably would have been available if the hearsay statement had been trustworthy, the obvious self-interest in the deceased's statement, and the possibility of the workman's being inebriated when he made his statement, the court reasonably could have ruled that credulity could not be placed in the supporting hearsay evidence and that such evidence did not, therefore, constitute substantial evidence. Instead, after noting that the commission could "accept any evidence that is offered" under the New York Workmen's Compensation Act, the court laid down the rule that "still in the end there must be a residuum of legal evidence to support the claim before an award can be made." It therefore held that when substantial evidence is required, "hearsay testimony is not evidence."

The residuum rule is both logically unsound and administratively impractical. In a trial before a lay jury, hearsay admitted without objection is given its natural, probative effect and may be the sole support for a verdict. But under the residuum rule hearsay cannot support a decision by an expert administrator. The rule ignores the reliability of technically incompetent evidence, rendering all such evidence ineffective unless corroborated. However, if corroborated, regardless of how slight the legal evidence, the same hearsay evidence will provide the substantial evidence needed to support the administrative finding.

This rule may also become a trap for the unwary, particularly where the hearing officer is not expert in the rules of evidence or where the parties are not represented by counsel. In fact it encourages trial examiners to apply the hearsay rule and exclude probative evidence in order to avoid possible error. In its instinctive protection of fairness in administrative hearings, through assuring that the decision is supported by evidence subject to confrontation and cross-examination, the residuum rule seems unassailable. What it fails to consider, however, is that much "legal" evidence within the hearsay exceptions is equally untested. Yet the latter is accepted even in jury trials because of its probable reliability. Consequently, the residuum rule's mechanical prohibition against uncorroborated hearsay is unsound. Its sound objectives can be secured through the sensitivity of hearing officers and the wise application of the substantial evidence test which measures the quantity and quality of the supporting evidence regardless of its category or label.

The residuum rule is not accepted by most federal courts. The states are still divided over its validity.

4. OPINION EVIDENCE AND EXPERT TESTIMONY

The presentation of expert and nonexpert opinions is increasingly common in administrative hearings. Medical issues arising in workmen's compensation claims are often complex, technical, and beyond the knowledge of either the hearing officer or the agency. An administrative decision to license an electric plant, to locate a public housing project, to discontinue a bus line, or to grant a liquor license frequently evokes strong community concern. The public views advanced are likely to be expressed in terms of opinion and to include reference to the views of others. To deny the public an opportunity to testify is to invite public rejection of the agency decision.

The general admissibility of expert and nonexpert testimony in administrative hearings is no longer open to question, but doubt still exists regarding the weight an expert's views should be given. For a time agencies and reviewing courts followed early judicial reasoning and refused to hear expert testimony on the very question that the agency was created to decide. Other courts took the position that it would be unfair for an agency to rely on its own expertise or the expert testimony of its staff when their opinions were contradicted by outside experts. In rejecting these contradictory appeals to ignorance, courts now recognize legislative intention to establish expert agencies. Therefore, agency decisions which rely on the agency's own expertise are upheld when the respondent offers no contrary expert testimony or when expert testimony offered by staff members and outside experts conflicts. Some courts have gone even further and given excessive deference to the knowledge of the administrative agency by upholding its decisions in the face of uncontradicted expert testimony to the contrary. However, the demands of fairness are now generally accepted, and an agency seeking to rely on its expertise must present expert testimony subject to cross-examination on the record or give the respondent fair notification that official notice will be taken of such "facts." See Davis & Randall, Inc. v. United States, 219 F. Supp. 673 (W.D.N.Y.1963) (Friendly, J.).

Perhaps because of this very limited judicial supervision, agency reliance on opinion and expert testimony often is at best vacillating and at worst irresponsible. Again the FTC's false advertising hearings are revealing and illustrative. To prove that an advertisement is false or deceptive, government counsel must show that the advertisement made a promise which respondent's product or service failed to meet. In other words, the agency must show what the consuming public understood from the advertisement.

The obvious method of proof would seem to be a scientific survey exploring the reactions of those who either relied upon the advertisement or were within the target area and could have been affected by it. Such surveys are rarely relied upon in Commission hearings; even when used, they are usually questionable samplings prepared at the behest of one partisan. Instead, the parties rely on a number of less significant factors: the Commission's experience and expertise, thereby adopting what is more accurately described as the "hunch" or "intuitive" approach; dictionary definitions which tell only the possible or preferred interpretation of words used in an advertisement, not how they are actually understood; trade understandings which are hardly reflective of consumer perception; or the opinions of a parade of consumer witnesses, testimony which needlessly prolongs the hearing and demonstrates only that somewhere, somehow, inventive counsel may find someone who will interpret an ad as counsel desires. Despite criticism of these practices, little change is discernible. On the other hand, if agencies were required to try cases quickly and to enforce their decisions meaningfully—developments which public pressures may demand—the agencies would be forced to make expert opinion readily available to all parties and to develop routine procedures for validating expert views.

5. EXCLUSION OF PRIVILEGED TESTIMONY

Witnesses in administrative hearings have the same general duty to give testimony which is incumbent on all citizens in judicial trials. Because the demand comes from the community as a whole, rather than from the parties, and because the obligation is essential to any search for justice, privileges of exemption from this duty are exceptional. Read literally, the APA's provision in section 7(c), that "[a]ny oral or documentary evidence may be received" (5 U.S. C.A. § 556(d)), authorizes the receipt of privileged evidence in administrative hearings. Nevertheless, administrative hearings have generally followed the judicial lead in recognizing several exceptions to this obligation to testify. Such exceptions are of two kinds. A few, such as the exclusion of illegally obtained evidence and the assertion of the right against self-incrimination, are based upon constitutional commands. Others, such as the privileges protecting attorney-client and marital communications, are founded upon the need to protect interests without constitutional dimension yet these relationships have sufficient social importance to warrant the sacrifice of full factual disclosure.

On the federal level, neither the Congress nor the agencies have focused on whether administrative agencies must recognize testimonial privileges not constitutionally required. In a leading case concerning the enforcement of an SEC subpoena, Judge Learned Hand expressly assumed that agency proceedings are "subject to the same testimonial privileges as judicial proceedings." McMann v. SEC, 87 F.2d 377, 378 (2d Cir. 1937). Agencies have generally accorded privileged treatment to communications between attorney and client, physician and patient, and husband and wife. But they have not been anxious to extend such privileges. For example, the accountant-client privilege recognized by a few states has not been accepted by federal agencies. Business secrets have been protected grudgingly, although agencies have become more sophisticated in recent years in protecting both the witness and the adjudicative process by *in camera* receipt of sensitive data.

Claims of privilege for government secrets are particularly important in administrative hearings. Any attempt to probe the government's case by discovery, subpoena of agency witnesses, or cross-examination is quickly met by claims that the information sought is privileged. Actually the government secrets privilege is asserted as an umbrella for three types of information: state secrets involving military or diplomatic information; requests that executive officers testify; and official government information which may range from the identity of informers and internal management materials to staff studies unrelated to any litigation. Only the third (omnibus) exception has special significance for administrative adjudications; the judicial rules applicable to state secrets and executive testimony are routinely followed in agency hearings.

Exculpatory information in an agency's possession or file data which may aid respondent's preparation or presentation of his case must be disclosed by the agency. The agency's alternative is to drop the prosecution against the respondent. Anything less violates the command of procedural due process which every adjudication must observe. But beyond this simple generalization which no one seriously disputes, it is unclear just what the duty to disclose includes. When does information become exculpatory? Can criteria be developed, or is this subject akin to obscenity and seemingly beyond anything but the vaguest definition? Is the duty limited to government counsel or does a corresponding duty apply to nonparties, especially when the latter

are the unseen de facto charging parties? Should
a respondent have a correlative obligation to disclose incriminating data since the proceedings
are civil and, at least as to corporate respondents, there is no right against self-incrimination?
Even if these questions can be answered satis-
factorily, what procedures should be adopted to
assure that exculpatory data is revealed? Although the cases still reflect only a glimmer of
concern for such disclosure, as agencies further
develop summary techniques or impose upon respondent the burden of proving its innocence—as
the demands for a cleaner environment and for
fairer business-consumer relations will require—
these questions should receive increasing attention.

6. PRESENTATION OF CASE: BURDEN OF PROOF AND PRESUMPTIONS

The customary common law rule that the
moving party has the burden of proof—including
not only the burden of going forward but also the
burden of persuasion—is generally observed in
administrative hearings. Section 7(c) of the
APA, for example, provides: "Except as otherwise provided by statute, the proponent of a rule
or order has the burden of proof." 5 U.S.C.A. §
556(d). In most hearings the burden of persuasion is met by the usual civil case standard of

"a preponderance of the evidence." However, where grave issues of personal security are at stake in an administrative hearing as in a deportation proceeding, the Supreme Court has imposed the equity standard that the government establish its allegations by "clear, unequivocal, and convincing evidence." Woodby v. Immigration & Naturalization Service, 385 U.S. 276, 87 S.Ct. 483 (1966).

Increasingly, the courts are also employing the substantial evidence standard to impose a special burden of proof on administrative agencies distributing compensation benefits. A series of cases involving social security and workmen's compensation proceedings have required that the agency accept the claimant's uncontroverted evidence even though the claimant has the burden of proof. E. g., Young & Co. v. Shea, 397 F.2d 185 (5th Cir. 1968), cert. denied, 395 U.S. 920, 89 S.Ct. 1771 (1968). Nor can these cases be explained away on the grounds of judicial acceptance of uncontradicted medical testimony in support of the claim, since the agencies are also dealing with malingering and false claims. On the other hand, reviewing courts are more concerned with the remedial, risk-spreading purposes of the statutes and the comparative inability of the claimant to present additional proof. Similar tendencies occasionally appear in such diverse areas as police suspension matters and draft exemption cases where the courts have given increasing scrutiny to the overall fairness of administrative adjudications. It would seem safe to predict the spread of this tendency to less formalized adjudications where the agency deals with an individual's liberties or claims.

These cases can also be viewed as establishing a presumption in certain administrative adjudications since they affect the burden of proof. The history of workmen's compensation illustrates this alternative analysis. Although many state acts have created a presumption in favor of the claimant, several state courts formerly gave these acts no such effect. In interpreting a federal compensation act in Del Vecchio v. Bowers, 296 U.S. 280, 56 S.Ct. 190 (1935), the Supreme Court held that this "benefit" presumption was sufficient to carry claimant's burden of persuasion in the absence of opposing evidence. However, once rebuttal evidence is introduced, the statutory presumption is overcome, and the agency must decide the case solely on the evidence in the record.* Similar analysis supports

* This also illustrates that problems of burden of proof are, in essence, often questions of substantive law. 2 K. C. Davis, Administrative Law Treatise § 14.14, at 328 (1958); see Republic Aviation Corp. v. NLRB, 324 U.S. 793, 65 S.Ct. 982 (1945); 2 K. C. Davis, supra § 15.04, at 372–73.

the presumption of the correctness of official administrative action.

On the other hand, precisely the opposite trend is beginning to surface in administrative adjudications where the activities of business respondents are tested. For example, an advertiser now has the burden of establishing any advertising claim, and if it is the type of claim whose truth can be determined only by scientific tests—for example, a claim that respondent's tires will stop a car 25 percent more quickly than other tires— the advertiser's fully-documented proof must *antedate* the representation; the prosecuting agency need only show that the claim was made. As increasing weight is given to the public interest in fair dealing and in a healthier environment, we can expect further developments either imposing strict liability on certain business activities or requiring that the business establish by substantial evidence that its practices should not be prohibited.

7. PRESENTATION OF CASE: WRITTEN EVIDENCE AND CROSS–EXAMINATION

Perhaps the most distinctive feature of many administrative hearings, particularly in contrast to nonjury trials, is the substitution of written evidence for oral testimony. This written evidence takes several forms. In its simplest and least productive aspect, some witnesses appear, if at all, simply for cross-examination, with the written questions and answers read into the record in lieu of the usual oral question-answer format. This "canned dialogue" has been savagely and justly criticized as an abomination leading to the withholding of the true facts from the hearing examiner and assuring that the case will be decided on grounds other than the evidence in the record. But if applied more sensitively, written evidence can expedite and simplify formal administrative proceedings through reducing the controversy to verified written statements which are then exchanged by the parties for the purpose of rebuttal. Federal administrative agencies have frequently relied upon this technique; the ICC has done so for almost half a century. With the cooperation of the parties, this procedure can result in greater precision than where the facts are presented orally.

Written evidence has been relied upon most successfully in rate or price control proceedings, where economic and expert analysis rather than sensorily-perceived phenomena provide the bulk of the evidence. Credibility based upon conflicting stories relating what each witness observed is seldom involved. Often the advance preparation of written evidence is limited to the contentions of the party having the burden of proof; in others the opposing party's evidence is included. The elimination of surprise cannot be objected to since surprise has no proper place in the hearing when credibility is not in issue. Cross-examination is not used to establish a party's case. Its major purpose here is "not to reduce . . . [the expert] witness to a shattered hulk by the admission of error, but to explore all of the considerations entering into what must remain a matter of judgment." See Selected Reports of the Administrative Conference of the United States 1961–62, S.Doc.No. 24, 88th Cong., 1st Sess. 92 (1963).

As explained by the Second Interim Administrative Conference, the benefits of written evidence are manifold:

> (1) [the] exchange of written evidence facilitates settlement techniques in situations in which there is staff participation; (2) the hearing examiner, after studying the direct evidence of the parties prior to hearing, can participate in the case in an intelligent fashion, leading to more effective use of conference techniques and more informed rulings at the hearing; (3) in a substantial number of cases, particularly those of less moment, the parties may be satisfied with their written presentations, and an oral hear-

ing becomes unnecessary; and (4) the efforts of the parties at the oral hearing, if one is necessary, are confined to clarifying the major issues through informed cross-examination. Properly handled, written procedures should result in a more adequate record being produced in a shorter space of time. (Id. at 93.)

Section 7(c) of the APA recognizes the propriety of written presentations with only limited cross-examination: "In rule making or determining claims for money or benefits or applications for initial licenses an agency may, when a party will not be prejudiced thereby, adopt procedures for the submission of all or part of the evidence in written form." 5 U.S.C.A. § 556(d). While denying the broad application of their recommendation to all adjudications, others have suggested the use of written presentations by any agency in a type of proceeding where the interest of any party is not prejudiced. Existing case authority on the point supports this conclusion. See Yakus v. United States, 321 U.S. 414, 64 S.Ct. 660 (1944).

Where cross-examination is necessary for protection against untrustworthy evidence, it cannot be avoided. Section 7(c) of the APA specifically preserves the right of cross-examination in agency adjudications: "A party is entitled . . .

to conduct such cross-examination as may be required for a full and true disclosure of the facts." 5 U.S.C.A. § 556(d). Through this provision the APA recognizes one of the fundamentals of a fair hearing—namely, a reasonable opportunity to test and controvert adverse evidence whether or not such evidence is a statement of opinion, observation, or consideration of the witness. Cross-examination has several potential uses: to bring out matters left untouched by direct examination; to test the accuracy of a witness' perception as well as his ability to observe; to probe his truthfulness; to question his memory and narration; and to expose the basis of any opinions he has expressed. In other words, "cross-examination is a means of getting at the truth; it is not truth itself." However, unless credibility is directly in issue—and then only on occasion—cross-examination invariably does no more than demonstrate forensic talent or score trial points irrelevant to the final decision. As an experienced agency practitioner, now an eminent federal judge, has observed: "Only rarely . . . can you accomplish something devastating on cross-examining an expert. More often it is love's labor lost."

Perception of this point is the key to a reconciliation of the right of cross-examination with the seemingly inconsistent administrative practice of relying on hearsay testimony and written evidence whether or not the declarant is unavailable. The legislative history of the APA clearly indicates that Congress was seeking to draw a line between an unlimited right of unnecessary cross-examination and a reasonable opportunity to test opposing evidence. The test, stated abstractly, is that cross-examination must be allowed when it is required for determining the truth. If witness veracity and demeanor are not critical, there is no requirement for cross-examination so long as sufficient opportunity for rebuttal exists; if credibility is a key factor, and the objecting party can show that the absence of cross-examination of the witness may have prejudiced his case, the denial of cross-examination could be fatal to an agency decision. See Richardson v. Perales, 402 U.S. 389, 91 S.Ct. 1420 (1971). Statistical compilations and surveys are admissible only if the person responsible for—and having full knowledge of the preparation of—the exhibit is available. In addition, the raw data upon which the exhibit is based should be available to the opposing party.

Finally, administrative agencies are required to apply the "Jencks rule"—namely, that after a government witness has testified, the prosecution must disclose prior statements by the witness relating to his testimony. Compare Jencks

v. United States, 353 U.S. 657, 77 S.Ct. 1007
(1957), with NLRB v. Adhesive Prods. Corp.,
258 F.2d 403 (2d Cir. 1958) and Communist
Party of the United States v. Subversive Activities Cont. Bd., 254 F.2d 314 (D.C. Cir. 1958).
Application of this rule in agency hearings has
been riddled with controversy. The Administrative Conference has offered this sensible solution—that prior statements be made available
to the respondent at the prehearing conference.
Recommendation No. 21—Discovery in Agency
Adjudication (adopted June 3, 1970). If this
view is adopted, the question will no longer be
one of evidence but of discovery.

C. NONRECORD EVIDENCE AND OFFICIAL NOTICE

Official notice, like its judicial notice counterpart, involves reliance by the presiding officer—
in this case, the hearing examiner—on extra-record information. That is, the examiner in making a decision relies upon facts and opinions not
supported by evidence "on the record." Official
notice, however, is distinguishable from judicial
notice in several respects. First, a specific procedure has been established to receive extra-record facts, with the parties receiving notice and
an opportunity to rebut the "noticed" facts. Second, extra-record facts usually have first been

developed by the agency's expert staff or accumulated from previous agency decisions. But official notice is not limited to information in agency files. In fact, it is often taken at the initiative of one of the parties. Third, agency recognition of extra-record facts is clearly not limited to either "indisputable" or "disputable" facts. Rather, official notice may extend to almost any information useful in deciding the adjudication as long as elemental fairness is observed.

On the other hand, in administrative adjudication, official notice is frequently confused with the process of decision-making. In reaching a conclusion, the examiner or agency may rely on its special skills, whether they include particular expertise in engineering, economics, medicine, or electricity, just as a judge may freely use his legal skills in reading statutes and applying decided cases in the preparation of his opinion. But such evaluations are not within the concept of official notice. Official notice is concerned with the *process of proof,* not with the *evaluation of evidence.* The difference between an administrative tribunal's use of nonrecord information included in its expert knowledge, as a substitute for evidence or notice, and its application of its background in evaluating and drawing conclusions from the evidence that is in the record, is primarily a difference of degree rather than of kind.

In principle, reliance upon the examiner's knowledge in the process of proof is permissible only within the confines of official notice, whereas the examiner's use of his experience in evaluating "proof" that has been offered is not only unavoidable but, indeed, desirable. The troublesome problem, as with most questions of law, is that a fine line cannot be drawn with precision. One commentator explained the point as follows:

> When the State Liquor Authority concludes, from evidence in the record as to the size of food bills and gas bills paid (in relation to the volume of liquor business), that the holder of a restaurant liquor license is not conducting a *bona fide* restaurant, is the Authority using its experience and knowledge to evaluate and draw conclusions from the evidence, or is it using its experience and knowledge as a substitute for further evidence as to the normal relation of the size of food and gas bills to the volume of food business? . . . My own view is that . . . the procedure described is permissible [evaluation]; but until the courts have decided specific questions of this character, it is impossible to anticipate with any certainty what their decision would be. (R. Benjamin, 1 Administrative Adjudication in the State of New York 212 (1942).)

Beyond this or other examples, little guidance can be offered.

The primary thrust behind official notice is to simplify or ease the process of proof. Where facts are known or can be safely assumed, the process of proving what is already known is both time consuming and unduly formal. When facts have been proven before, further proof becomes tiresome, redundant, and lacking in common sense. At times even the obvious could be difficult or time-consuming to prove without affecting the final result which was never in doubt. Moreover, administrative agencies were often created to become repositories of knowledge and experience. It would defeat their existence to require adherence to traditional methods of proof when alternative and equally fair methods are readily available. On the other hand, in developing an alternative method it is necessary to safeguard the elements of a fair trial preserved by the traditional forms of proof. The Attorney General's Committee accurately summarized the need:

> The parties, then, are entitled to be apprised of the data upon which the agency is acting. They are entitled not only to refute but, what in this situation is usually more important, to supplement, explain, and give different perspective to the facts upon which the

agency relies. In addition, upon judicial review, the court must be informed of what facts the agency has utilized in order that the existence of supporting evidence may be ascertained.

Congress sought to recognize and reconcile these concerns by a single sentence in section 7(c) of the APA: "When an agency decision rests on official notice of a material fact not appearing in the evidence in the record, a party is entitled, on timely request, to an opportunity to show the contrary." 5 U.S.C.A. § 556(e).

The procedure is simple. Official notice is a means by which an agency can avoid hearing further evidence on a material fact in the case if it notifies the parties that unless they prove to the contrary the agency's findings will include that particular fact and allows the parties an opportunity to present contrary evidence. For example, after hearing dozens of cases indicating that consumers preferred American to foreign-made goods—and holding, therefore, that a failure to disclose the foreign origin of these goods was a false and deceptive act—the FTC advised in Manco Watch Strap Co., 60 F.T.C. 495 (1962) that it would not hear evidence on this issue in the future. Then, in subsequent cases where the FTC took official notice and the respondents could not prove that American consumers preferred either foreign goods or that the consumers had no particular preference, the Commission upheld orders barring sales of goods not bearing the requisite disclosures. On the other hand, where a respondent showed that consumers preferred French over American perfumes, for example, the "noticed finding" did not apply.

Practically, then, the primary effect of taking official notice is to transfer the burden of proof on that material fact—usually from the agency to the respondent. The significance of this tactic varies in proportion to the difficulty of the proponent in establishing that fact originally and the cost and effort of the opponent in disproving it. In most instances where agencies have taken official notice, the former costs have been slight since the result has seemed obvious. Where the fact is less obvious, however, these costs could prove substantial.

The academic controversy over official notice has centered upon sterile attempts to categorize the types of facts which can be officially noticed. The APA's guidance is slender; it merely sets forth the procedure which must be followed for taking notice of "material facts." By omission it appears to suggest that facts which are not material can be noticed in the manner of a judge at a judicial trial, but it does not tell how to determine which facts are material and must therefore be noticed or proved.

The Attorney General's Committee on Administrative Procedure suggested a distinction between "litigation" and "nonlitigation" facts:

> If information has come to an agency's attention in the course of investigation of the pending case, it should be adduced only by the ordinary process. . . . But if the information has been developed in the usual course of business of the agency, if it has emerged from numerous cases, if it has become a part of the factual equipment of the administrators, it seems undesirable for the agencies to remain oblivious of their own experience [and, they should take notice of such facts].

Professor Davis, on the other hand, rejects the notion that significance could be attached to the time when the factual data were collected. As an alternative to the Committee rule, he asserts that legislative facts (the general facts not related to particular parties) usually need not be brought into the record by official notice; where critical, a party should be able to challenge them by brief and argument. He contends that adjudicative facts (who did what, where, when, and with what motive or intent), on the other hand, must be brought into the record—unless they are indisputable—either through direct proof or by official notice. Nothing less will meet the cardinal principles of a fair hearing—notice and an opportunity to test and rebut opposing evidence. Whether such adjudicative facts can be officially noticed or must be established by direct proof depends, he says, on three variables: How close the facts are to the center of the controversy; the extent to which the facts are adjudicative or legislative; and the degree to which the facts are certain. As the adjudicative facts move closer to the basic issues of the hearing, relate to the parties, and are disputed, the usual methods of proof must be observed; as they move in the opposite direction, official notice is permissible. 2 K. C. Davis, Administrative Law Treatise ch. 15 (1958, Supp. 1970).

The difficulty with Davis' analysis lies not in his categories, which are original and helpful, but rather that many cases fall outside his definitions. A sampling of cases illustrates this point. The existence of the Great Depression is a "legislative" fact which an agency can include in its findings without notice to the parties, but a specific price trend, also a general legislative fact, cannot be used to update the figures in the record without notice to the parties. Compare Ohio Bell Tel. Co. v. Public Util. Comm'n, 301 U.S. 292, 57 S.Ct. 724 (1937), with West Ohio Gas Co. v. Public Util. Comm'n, 294 U.S. 63, 68, 55 S.Ct. 316, 319 (1935). Since a specific price trend can be readily verified, taking notice is appropriate; the burden of proving any substantial error is not likely to be significant. Similarly, several courts have upheld agencies' official notice of scientific data, technical facts, and articles in academic journals, although other courts contend that this places too great a burden on the opponent to refute the "noticed evidence."

Of greater consequence is the fact that reliance upon Davis' categories distracts from the central question of fairness—that is, is it fair in the particular hearing to take official notice and to *transfer the burden of proof* to the opposing party? Two cases involving the use of the record of a related hearing, which reached opposite results, are perhaps the clearest examples of this suggested "fairness of the transfer of the burden of proof" analysis. In United States v. Pierce Auto Freight Lines, Inc., 327 U.S. 515, 66 S.Ct. 687 (1946), the ICC held two separate hearings on competing applications for truck service between San Francisco and Portland. Each applicant intervened in the other hearing, but the cases were not consolidated (*Ashbacker* not being applicable because the number of available licenses was not limited). In reaching its decision, the Commission relied on evidence appearing in only one record. This procedure was upheld because both applicants were parties to both proceedings and both had ample opportunity to present evidence, to cross-examine witnesses, and otherwise to protect their interests.

In the second case, Dayco Corp. v. FTC, 362 F.2d 180 (6th Cir. 1966), the FTC sought to take official notice of the distribution system and of practices used by the respondent, a manufacturer of auto replacement parts, since the system had been the subject of a prior proceeding. That prior proceeding, in which respondent was only a witness, was brought against his customers. The court ruled that the FTC's attempt to take official notice of these "adjudicative" facts from the first proceeding was improper because the manufacturer was not a party, but only a witness, to the prior proceeding. The agency had asserted that its reliance on prior knowledge merely shifted the burden of going forward to respondent and this burden (of correcting any FTC errors in describing respondent's distribution system) was minimal when compared with the cost of proving these same facts again. The FTC's argument was not persuasive. If the agency merely sought to shift the burden of going forward, it could have introduced the prior record as reliable hearsay evidence subject to rebuttal or as written evidence with an offer to make the witnesses available for cross-examination. If handled in this manner—rather than under the of-

ficial notice rubric—the fact trier would still
have to determine whether the prior record accurately portrayed respondent's distribution system. The court may also have perceived that
there was no compelling need to approve the
Commission's proposal since the FTC could (and
should) have avoided the burden of re-proof by
joining the respondent as a party in the first
proceeding. Official notice, in other words, is
not properly a procedural device to avoid the requirement of section 7(c) of the APA that the
moving party has the burden of proof. If that
burden is to be placed on respondent as a condition of doing business, it should be accomplished
openly through a shift in substantive policy rather than covertly by manipulation of procedural
devices.

D. THE PRESIDING OFFICER AND THE
DECISIONAL PROCESS

Although agency enabling acts generally state
that the head of the agency "shall decide," the
pressures of practical administration require that
subordinates be delegated the authority to decide
most matters initially. Heads of agencies—cabi-
net officers, commissioners, single officer administrators—must be free to concentrate on larger
and more important questions of policy and practice. Subordinates, namely hearing examiners,

should sift the facts, decide preliminary procedural questions, and make the initial determinations that as a practical matter finally decide all but the most important cases.

At one time, the authority of an agency to redelegate any of its powers was questioned. In fact, the Supreme Court once went so far as to hold that the power to sign and issue a subpoena (which in a federal court is issued by a clerk at the request of a party) could be exercised only by the agency head—in this case by the Wage-Hour Administrator—even though his office issued over 6,000 subpoenas annually. Cudahy Packing Co. v. Holland, 315 U.S. 357, 62 S.Ct. 651 (1942). The realities of administrative life quickly altered judicial attitudes, and under the various reorganization acts, by which the President (subject to congressional veto) can restructure federal agencies and departments, the President has changed the law specifically to allow redelegation of most assigned functions. Consequently, the problem of "subdelegation" is, in reality, of historical interest only.

More important is the status of the hearing examiner, the presiding officer in most adjudications (and in all subject to the APA). The selection and retention of qualified examiners is, in the words of the Attorney General's Committee on Administrative Procedure 30 years ago, "the heart of formal administrative adjudication." At one time, hearing examiners were an odd assortment of political appointees and untrained personnel assigned to monitor the proceedings. They were "presiding officers" in the sense that they policed the receipt of evidence and certified the record, often without making any findings or decision. Even when they did render an initial decision, their rulings were not final, and in any case their views were usually ignored. Nor surprisingly, examiners were held in low esteem as a group and the parties assailed their lack of independence and fairness.

As a result of the adoption of the APA in 1946, the status and stature of federal examiners was, after some unseemly squabbles, enhanced. Their salaries were raised substantially, their selection was professionalized, and their independence from agency domination was assured by section 11 of the APA. 5 U.S.C.A. §§ 1305, 3105, 3344, 5352, 7521. Examiners now have tenure, can be assigned only those tasks which are consistent with their judicial stature, and decide cases in the name of the agency unless an appeal is filed. That is, the examiner is now the adjudicator, not just the agency's policeman; however, he does not have the mystique or independent force of a presidentially appointed federal district judge.

The examiner's function is twofold: to conduct the hearings, and to render an initial or recommended decision. In this connection, section 7 (b) of the APA delegates the necessary authority directly to the examiner, including the power to issue subpoenas, to rule on evidentiary matters, and to decide the case initially. 5 U.S.C.A. § 556(c). Since agencies are not passive recipients of cases in the adversarial process, the examiner has an even greater responsibility than a trial judge to exercise his affirmative duty of developing a record that fully reveals the facts necessary to a sound decision yet is not overly long or redundant.

On the other hand, the examiner's position is not just limited by the provision of section 8(a) of the APA that on "review of the initial decision, the agency has all the powers which it would have in making the initial decision except as it may limit the issues on notice or by rule. 5 U.S.C.A. § 557(b). It is, rather, that all participants in agency proceedings recognize that it is the agency which sets policy. In other words, it, not the examiner, is the final arbiter and policy maker. Nevertheless, as the quality of the examiner corps improves and as agencies increasingly delegate power to them (e. g., by allowing only exceptional interlocutory appeals, by reviewing only a selected number of cases), the power, prestige and (undoubtedly) pay of hearing examiners will continue to rise.

The deference, if any, which the agency must pay to the examiner's findings and conclusions is a matter of some continuing controversy. Since the ultimate decision is the agency's and since section 8(a) of the APA preserves for the agency "all the powers which it would have in making the initial decision," agency review of an initial decision is not confined to determining whether the examiner's decision is supported by substantial evidence. That is to say, the agency is required to render what it deems to be the "correct" decision, and not just to act as a reviewing court obliged to approve a "permissible" decision. Universal Camera Corp. v. NLRB, 340 U.S. 474, 71 S.Ct. 456 (1951).

However, the examiner's findings and conclusions are part of the record and cannot be ignored by the agency. In addition, where demeanor evidence is critical to the decision, the examiner's conclusion on the credibility of a witness is entitled to "special weight." But it is still the agency's function to determine the correctness of the decision, and if it can adequately explain why the record supports its conclusion, a reviewing court should uphold the agency even though the agency decision reversed an examiner "who saw the witnesses." See FCC v. Allentown

Broadcasting Corp., 349 U.S. 358, 75 S.Ct. 855 (1955).

The volume of agency business and the location of ultimate responsibility for decisions of law and policy (and, under section 8(a) of the APA, of the facts) in the agency head raises several problems. Must the agency head hear the testimony, or at least read the entire record, before making his decision? Can a party inquire into the decisional processes to determine whether the agency head has in fact read the record or the cited portions? Can the agency decision maker consult with the staff before making his decision? Should the agency head who decides the case be required to write the opinion—or should the opinion in any case be issued in his name? These and similar questions involve what has been denominated the question of "institutional decision making."

Behind these questions lies the conflict between the personalized decision so common in the common law court and the organizational or management approach relied upon by large companies in a complex economy. The issue is what must the "man at the top" do personally to satisfy the constitutional demand of due process as well as the needs of sound administration. On the one hand, group decision making permits efficient use of available skills and expertise, takes advantage of the check and balance garnered by soliciting several views, and assures that a large volume of work will be treated uniformly. The drawbacks, however, are the lessened responsibility resulting from an anonymous decision (no one's feet are "held to the fire"), and the possibility that the decider relied upon nonrecord information frustrating the parties' opportunity for a hearing. Obviously, some compromises must be made, although it is clear that extra record facts (but not ideas) which would otherwise have to be proved or be subject to official notice should not be supplied ex parte.

As the hearing examiner has gained status, as the volume of agency business has increased geometrically, and as the judicialization of decision making has continued, agencies have been forced —as the courts have conceded—to rely upon their staffs in deciding cases and in announcing their decisions. Thus, to answer the questions posed above, it is now clear (1) that deciding officers may make findings of fact based upon a reading of the record (i. e., without actually hearing the witnesses testify); (2) that the deciding officer need not read the entire record; (3) that the mental processes of the deciding officer (i. e., the mechanics by which he reaches his decision) not revealed by the opinion itself cannot be probed by the parties; (4) that agency heads may engage in ex parte consultations with noninvestigative and nonprosecutorial staff members, except that hearing examiners are forbidden from consulting "any person or party on any *fact* in issue," 5 U.S.C.A. § 554(d); and (5) that opinion writing can be delegated to staff members (however, important policy opinions should be closely supervised or written by agency members). Upon reflection, none of these propositions seems particularly startling.

E. BIAS AND INFLUENCE

The essence of an opportunity to be heard in an adjudication, as in a trial before a court or jury, is a hearing before a fair and unbiased tribunal. This does not mean that the trier of fact must be empty headed as well as open minded. He may, in fact is expected to, have preconceived views on law and policy. That is often the purpose of the legislature's assignment of the subject matter to an administrative tribunal in the first instance. What is sought, and what freedom from bias or prejudice means in a legal sense, is not that the hearing examiner or agency member is indifferent but rather that he be *impartial*. That is, the quasi-judicial officer must (a) not have prejudged the issues of fact about the parties in the case before him; (b) not have a personal bias or prejudice toward the parties which might impede his ability to judge issues of fact fairly; and (c) not have a personal interest whereby he stands to gain or lose from the outcome. In each of these situations the underlying concern is that the trier could not render a verdict on the merits in accordance with the facts in the record. An expressed view demonstrating a closed mind or even a predisposition toward one view of the facts or the parties suggests that a fair verdict may be denied. Likewise no one should be the judge of his own cause. In applying these tests, the standard is not proof of prejudgment or interest beyond a reasonable doubt, but rather do the facts make it likely that a fair trial is unavailable *or* do they give an appearance of unfairness. The overriding concern is for fairness; any taint of unfairness impairs the entire administrative process.

None of these principles is new or unique to administrative law. They have been applied for generations in the common law courts. What is different about administrative tribunals is their admitted "self interest" in a specific law or policy. The Labor Board, for example, was established to protect labor unions and to promote collective bargaining. Charges of unfair labor practices were assigned for hearing before the NLRB because the courts had previously demonstrated a strong anti-union or management sympathy.

Congress was concerned that its mandate would be frustrated if labor cases were tried by federal district judges. Thus, the Board was created to give unions and their members an understanding hearing. Management, not surprisingly, took a different view of the fairness of these new procedures. However, when challenged, the Supreme Court has repeatedly held that bias in the sense of a crystallized point of view on law or policy is not ground for disqualification. E. g., FTC v. Cement Institute, 333 U.S. 683, 68 S.Ct. 793 (1948). It follows also that when an examiner (or agency) makes an erroneous ruling which is subsequently reversed, the examiner (or agency) is not disqualified—just as reversal does not usually disqualify a trial judge—from hearing the case on remand. E. g., NLRB v. Donnelly Garment Co., 330 U.S. 219, 67 S.Ct. 756 (1947). As trained lawyers and impartial experts, examiners and agency members are expected to be able to exercise the intellectual self-discipline necessary to try the case anew with an open mind.

Once again the principles are easier to state than apply. What of the administrative official who has previously been involved as a staff member of a congressional committee investigating practices in a particular industry and later sits in judgment as a quasi-judicial member of an agency which is prosecuting one firm in the industry for an unfair method of competition? The Sixth Circuit held that such "particularized foreknowledge" of the facts, especially when it was acquired by the agency official (FTC commissioner) as an active participant in an accusatory congressional investigation, requires the administrator to recuse himself from the proceeding.   American Cyanamid Co. v. FTC, 363 F.2d 757 (6th Cir. 1966).   The D.C. Circuit went even farther in holding that due process commands the disqualification of an FTC commissioner from acting in his quasi-judicial capacity where, in a speech to a trade association, he named the respondent as one of several companies whose practices of "price fixing, price discrimination, and overriding commissions on TBA" were alleged to be "plagu[ing] you and we have challenged their legality."   Texaco, Inc. v. FTC, 336 F.2d 754 (D.C. Cir. 1964), vacated on other grounds, 381 U.S. 739, 85 S.Ct. 1798 (1965). These cases are distinct in the sense that they involve the appearance of prejudgment resulting from the administrator's official acts rather than from any personal relationship to the parties or the outcome.   Yet a quasi-judicial officer (or judge) is not precluded from deciding a case even though the facts and events are identical to a prior case he decided.   Perhaps, then, these cases also highlight a heightened judicial sensitivity to charges of governmental impropriety; only the barest implication of a fact prejudgment will support judicial disqualification. It has been suggested that these and other cases make it unnecessarily difficult for agency officials to make any but the blandest speeches or for staff personnel to be promoted to agency membership. In fact such concerns are overstated.

Occasionally, administrative boards are divided into groups, some members representing identified interests and others obliged to pursue an undifferentiated public interest. Typical, and perhaps most prominent, are the various wage-price boards established during the economic emergencies of recent wars and the postpartum period of the Vietnam conflict. Similar tripartite boards composed of labor, management and the public are commonly adopted to assure labor peace, such as the National Railroad Adjustment Board. In combining negotiation with adjudication, it is not expected that the partisan appointees to such panels shall do other than represent their constituents' interest. On the other hand, the standards of conduct normally applicable to quasi-judicial officers apply to the public members. The problem of institutionalized interest is most troublesome in connection with occupational licensing boards at state and local levels. They are frequently staffed on a part-time basis by industry members who have a pecuniary interest in "fencing out" competitors. In other situations, such a pecuniary interest would bar their participation, but no one else may have the competence to test a respondent's skills or to assess the charges. If no alternative is available, the attempt is to check potential bias by internal procedural safeguards (formalized procedures, strict judicial review, etc.). Further developments seem likely. See, e. g., Berryhill v. Gibson, 331 F.Supp. 122 (D.C.Ala.1971) (14th amendment bars revocation of an optometrist's license where the board is composed solely of private practitioners selected from trade association members).

Where several judges are available for assignment to a case within a judicial district, the problem of bias is readily resolved by the appointment of another judge to the case. At the first hearing stage in administrative proceedings, additional hearing examiners are also available. Where disqualification for alleged bias would immobilize the agency—for example, a single administrator exercises quasi-judicial power or a quorum would not otherwise be available—the overriding need for a decision requires that the administrative agency not be disqualified. This conclusion is generally denominated the rule of necessity. Its dangers are mitigated by invoking a more intensive test of review or, alternatively, by allowing de novo judicial consideration when the agency's expertise is not exclusive.

Finally, in contrast to the federal judicial procedure that when a trial judge's fairness is challenged his only function is to determine the adequacy (and not the truth) of the affidavit (28 U.S.C.A. § 144), a hearing examiner need not withdraw upon the mere filing of an affidavit of prejudice. Section 7(a) of the APA provides that he may either recuse himself voluntarily or be removed by the agency if it is convinced that cause exists. 5 U.S.C.A. § 556(b). However, the APA is silent on whether the decision to disqualify an agency member is solely a matter of his conscience as in the case of an appellate judge (except that a court reviewing the administrator's decision may require disqualification) or should be determined by his colleagues. Courts seem to prefer the latter alternative, but agency practice varies.

Another area of some difficulty is the control of outside influences on agency action. Obviously, influence peddling and covert contacts between deciding officials and only some of the parties on the merits are condemned. Like individual bias or prejudgment, they deprive the public and the parties of a fair decision developed upon a consideration of the record. On the other hand, legislative inquiries to the agency (invariably performed on behalf of constituents or friends indirectly seeking favorable results) are routine—although executive pressures are more suspect. Perhaps the first step in controlling such contacts was taken by the Fifth Circuit in Pillsbury Co. v. FTC, 354 F.2d 952 (5th Cir. 1966), when it held that an open congressional inquiry into how the law should be interpreted in a pending case constituted improper influence. The court's theory was that an administrator whose tenure is insecure (a seven year appointment) and whose agency is subject to annual appropriation review, might be unable to function impartially under overt congressional pressure. Whether the case reflects disenchantment with the particular agency or presages ever stricter limits against outside influence on quasi-judicial decision making remains unclear. See also D. C. Fed'n of Civic Ass'ns v. Volpe, 3 E.R.C. 1143 (D.C.Cir. Oct. 12, 1971), cert. denied, 92 S.Ct. 1290 (1972) (invalidating DOT decision authorizing bridge construction because of covert legislative pressure).

The basic point is unchanged, however. Administrative agencies, like other government bodies, face many influences. As the value of their decision to particular interests or groups increases—an inevitable byproduct of ever larger government coverage of all segments of the economy and society—the likelihood of direct or covert pressures will also increase. The thrust of most decisions is to impose tighter restraints on such influence; the aim is to expose ex parte contacts and to place reasonable boundaries on such extramural pressures.

F. COMBINATION OF FUNCTIONS

Intimately related to the decisional process and to questions of fairness is the fact that many (but far from all) administrative agencies combine a wide range of functions. Within one agency, the staff, examiners or members may investigate alleged infractions, prosecute those it believes to have violated a statute or regulation, and evaluate and judge the evidence submitted at a hearing which the agency itself has initiated. If it is improper for an examiner or judge to decide his own cause because of the potential for prejudice and appearance of bias, why, it is asked, should an agency be allowed to impose sanctions or deny substantial benefits where precisely the same situation occurs? Pecuniary interest is not the only basis for finding bias. As Justice Jackson accurately observed: "Men are more often bribed by their loyalties and ambitions than by money." United States v. Wunderlich, 342 U.S. 98, 103, 72 S.Ct. 154, 157 (1951).

This analysis ignores, however, that agencies typically are large organizations, not one or a few individuals. Maxims for judging the propriety of individual actions often make no sense when applied to a government or to one of its agencies. No one questions that the state in a criminal case investigates and prosecutes through the police and district attorney, provides defense counsel through the defender's office, supplies the law decider through the judge, and ascertains guilt or innocence through a paid jury. Similarly, even though a complaint may be issued in the name of an agency, organizational division of adjudicative from other administrative activities will satisfy basic procedural norms. Insulation of quasi-judicial officials (examiners, review boards, agency members) from ex parte contacts with the prosecuting staff and investigatory files was a necessary first step. The independence of the examiner was another. Organizational loyalties do not mean that hearing examiners invariably accept the prosecuting staff's version; and it is not uncommon for agencies to reject over one-third of the cases appealed to them (after the examiner has already dismissed the least convincing charges).*

---

* Statistics can be treacherous, however. Either party may appeal. A case may be dismissed on other (i.e., legal) grounds. Institutional bias, if any, may not necessarily be accurately reflected in actual numbers.

This is not to say, however, that complex problems are not involved or that agencies have adequately assured that adjudicatory processes are independent. FTC commissioners, for example, are actually given (and may read) the investigative file in determining whether to issue a complaint, even though they later may sit on the case as the final quasi-judicial authority (and their decision is constitutionally required to be limited to record evidence). Mistakes have also been made in the other direction. The Labor Board's prosecutorial function was separated from the NLRB in 1947. This separation, while not the total failure once asserted, is wasteful and seems to have led only to an uneasy truce between the General Counsel and the Board rather than protection of the adjudicatory process.

One recurring suggestion directed primarily at the administrative side of the combination of functions question is that it distracts the agency leadership from giving proper attention to the development of sound policy, and, conversely, that the agency members also do not have sufficient time to perform their adjudicatory function well. These conclusions often lead to recommendations that adjudicative functions be separated, that administrative courts be established to decide cases brought by agencies, and that agencies should be led by a single rather than a multimember body. Others respond that policy is most effectively developed by the flexible use of rulemaking and adjudication, and that the decision of whom, when and how to prosecute is often as much a policy function as how the decision is rendered.

G. FINDINGS, CONCLUSIONS AND REASONS

Section 8(b) of the APA requires that every adjudicatory decision must be accompanied by a statement of "findings and conclusions, and the reasons or basis therefor, on all the material issues of fact, law, or discretion presented on the record." 5 U.S.C.A. § 557(c). Administrators, in other words, are required to explain their decisions. The aim is to urge the agency to give careful rather than cursory consideration, to keep them within statutory bounds, to assist judicial review of agency decisions and to develop a body of available precedent. See, e. g., Citizens to Preserve Overton Park, Inc. v. Volpe, 401 U.S. 402, 91 S.Ct. 814 (1971). In part, of course, the only consequence is a meaningless verbal formalization—the boiler plate of the parties' briefs and the agency's decisions. On the other hand, unexplained administrative actions may be inexplicable and unjustifiable. As Judge Frank once stated so well: "[A]dministrative agencies, when acting judicially, have an obligation to be as articulate as practically possible. For no aspect of a democratic government should be mysterious."

CHAPTER XI

OBTAINING JUDICIAL REVIEW

A. METHODS OF REVIEW

At common law the courts developed a variety of techniques or remedies to allow judicial scrutiny of administrative action. The legislatures also authorized review of agency actions through enabling statutes establishing an agency and by broad statutes applicable to agencies generally. Judicial review focuses not only on agency applications for enforcement of its orders, but also on appeals by regulated persons to protest administrative action or inaction (e. g., direct review of the administrative order, application to enjoin or force administrative action, damage actions against the agency or administrator personally). The acute comment that "[t]he law of remedies against the United States is a complicated mosaic of judge-made rules and statutory enactments," applies with even greater force when state administrative review procedures are considered. Consequently, this analysis sweeps even more broadly than usual.

1. ENFORCEMENT OF ADMINISTRATIVE ORDERS

At one time administrative orders were not self-operative. If the respondent did not comply voluntarily, the agency had to bring a suit for enforcement. Even then the order was not binding until judicially enforced. In every instance, the respondent was assured judicial scrutiny of the order—whether it was properly made and within the scope of the agency's authority.

This two-step procedure—requiring proof before the agency of the violation and before the court of the regularity of the agency's proceeding—proved cumbersome and unnecessarily time-consuming. It required an agency to seek judicial enforcement and to meet the standards of judicial review even though the parties did not seriously object to the order. It also allowed the respondent which the agency had found to be violating the rule or regulation to continue the objectionable practices until the judicial order was issued. Once the agency's order was judicially approved, however, the court's order could be enforced by contempt procedures. Thus, enforcement was both too late and too harsh when it finally occurred. Reforms have now eliminated automatic judicial review. Except for the NLRB, most federal administrative orders are final unless appealed within a set time period (usually 60 days). In addition, failure to comply with an order is subject to statutory penalty. In other words, the order is self-executing unless the respondent takes immediate action to appeal.

2. OTHER STATUTORY REVIEW

Specific statutory provisions for enforcement of agency orders also provide for review at the request of the regulated party. In addition, general statutory review provisions—in particular, state administrative procedure acts—authorize judicial review of administrative action. It is unclear (and doubtful), however, whether section 10 of the APA is an independent grant of jurisdiction to review. Whatever the governing provisions, review is usually restricted to the record made in the hearing and the agency's ruling is "final" if supported by "substantial evidence on the whole record."

3. NONSTATUTORY REVIEW

Statutory review is not an exclusive alternative. It may not provide an adequate remedy. For example, it is usually limited to the record made at the administrative hearing. But review may be sought for failure to hold a hearing or for matters outside the record. Similarly, the party seeking review may seek damages or may want to prevent imminent or ongoing action.

Although the government enjoys sovereign immunity from suit, its officers and agents do not. They are answerable as private individuals for their actions, even if committed in the course of their official work. To recover damages, the plaintiff must show not only that the officer's action was not legally authorized, but also that the injury was a private wrong to the plaintiff. The officer usually seeks to justify his conduct by reference to the statute under which he was acting. This, of course focuses the issue upon the question for which review is sought: Was the administrator's conduct authorized under the circumstances? At one time, an officer acting within his colorable authority apparently could be held responsible for damages if his actions were malicious. However, concern that an administrator should not be subjected to the "constant dread of retaliation" for only doing his duty has resulted in severe limitations on this avenue of recovery. See, e. g., Barr v. Matteo, 360 U.S. 564, 572, 79 S.Ct. 1335, 1340 (1959). In any case, if recovery is allowed, it is limited by the officer's personal wealth (if any).

Yet it is manifestly unjust not to compensate an injury merely because it results from governmental rather than private action. Consequently, state and federal governments are increasingly waiving their sovereign immunity and accepting liability for the tortious or illegal conduct of their officers. In the past decade, many (perhaps even most) governmental immunities have been overturned by courts and legislatures. Such relief is not unlimited, however. For example, the Federal Tort Claims Act (28 U.S.C.A. §§ 1346, 1402, 1504, 2110, 2401–02, 2411–12, 2671–80) excludes liability for most wilful torts and any claims where the government employee has exercised due care or performed a discretionary function.

With these gaping holes in coverage, the private action for damages—against either the administrator or the agency—is generally inadequate. Uncompensated or unprotected victims of government action occasionally can rely on other alternatives, however. An equity injunction, often accompanied by a request for declaratory judgment, is the most common remedy. It rests on the same theory as a damage action; that is, it assumes that unless enjoined, the officer will commit acts entitling the complainant to damages. An injunction is the "catchall" remedy designed to prevent threatened irreparable injury for which there is no adequate remedy at law. Although there is increasing pressure upon the government to abandon all defenses of sovereign immunity and to rely instead upon a specific need for narrowly defined governmental exemptions, sovereign immunity may still apply and deny relief. Larson v. Domestic & Foreign Corp., 337 U.S. 682, 69 S.Ct. 1457 (1949).

Other remedies, relied upon mainly in the states, are the various prerogative writs inherited from the English system: certiorari (an order to the agency to certify its quasi-judicial record to the court for review—the counterpart of modern statutory review); mandamus (a command to an administrative officer to perform a duty—applicable if the action is "ministerial"; usually not available if it is "discretionary"); prohibition (an order enjoining the agency from exercising jurisdiction—ordinarily not available if later judicial review is adequate); and habeas corpus (an order to a government official detaining a person to explain and justify the legal basis for that detention).

B. REVIEWABILITY

A threshold question formerly of major significance and still applicable in divergent contexts, is whether any court has jurisdiction to review the administrator's action. In other words, does the court have jurisdiction over the subject matter of agency action, or is the action committed to the agency's discretion. The APA reflects a conflict between the desire to give the agency freedom to act and the competing interest to provide judicial protection of individual claims. The preamble to section 10 provides for review "except to the extent that . . . agency action is by law committed to agency discretion" while subsection 10(e) commands that the reviewing court shall "set aside agency action . . . found to be (A) arbitrary, capricious, an abuse of discretion, or otherwise not in accordance with law." 5 U.S.C.A. §§ 701, 706. It has been argued that the command of subsection 10(e) controls and only reasonably exercised discretion is committed to the agency; that is, the courts are obligated to hear every claim of abuse of agency discretion. This interpretation is strengthened by the argument that the individual interest in having the claim heard and the agency's long range interest in establishing the fairness of its proceedings outweigh any interest in effective, swift and economical enforcement. Others contend, more persuasively, that if the action is committed by law to agency discretion, then to that extent the agency's actions cannot be reviewed for abuse of discretion. There are a multitude of situations where judicial review is neither desirable nor practicable, including activity ranging from governmental operation of proprietary affairs to military activities. The case law supports this latter view. E. g., Panama Canal Co. v. Grace Line,

356 U.S. 309, 78 S.Ct. 752 (1958) (tolls set by government corporation not reviewable); Curran v. Laird, 420 F.2d 122 (D.C. Cir. 1969) (decision to use non-American vessels to transport military cargo to Vietnam not reviewable).

Nevertheless, the dominant view today is that a request for judicial review should be granted unless review is specifically precluded by statute (or other indication of legislative intent) or a special reason for nonreviewability exists. In other words, the presumption is that administrative action is reviewable. This presumption is spelled out most clearly in Abbott Laboratories v. Gardner, 387 U.S. 136, 87 S.Ct. 1507 (1967). The Court upheld an attempt by drug manufacturers to obtain anticipatory review—that is, preenforcement review—of FDA regulations for prescription drug labels. Its language is instructive: "[J]udicial review of a final agency action by an aggrieved person will not be cut off unless there is persuasive reason to believe that such was the purpose of Congress. . . . The legislative material elucidating that seminal act [the APA] manifests a congressional intention that it cover a broad spectrum of administrative actions . . . ." The APA's "generous review provisions" are to be given a "hospitable" interpretation. "[O]nly upon a showing of 'clear and convincing evidence' of a contrary legislative intent should the courts restrict access to judicial review." Stating that there is a presumption favoring review, however, indicates only a judicial attitude; it provides neither an answer nor a framework for analysis.

Equally inconclusive is the mere statement in a statute that there shall be no judicial review or that judicial review is available only at a specified (later) time. For example, whether a selective service order is reviewable prior to induction depends, in the first instance, upon the statutory authority of the administrator. In the draft cases, Congress clearly stated that review of Selective Service classifications is restricted to habeas corpus appeals (after induction) or criminal proceedings (after the draftee disobeys the induction order). However, such legislative restriction does not prevent review where a local Board's reclassification of student protesters is an obvious attempt to stifle dissent. The protection of First Amendment rights cannot be chilled by postponement of judicial review. Wolff v. Selective Service Local Board No. 16, 372 F.2d 817 (2d Cir. 1967). Nor can a divinity student be reclassified—in the face of a specifc statutory exemption—for returning his registration certificate as an expression of his opposition to the Vietnam war. In the case of the protesting divinity student, however, the Court did not rely upon the constitutional ground. It only held that since the Act does not authorize such classification the Board's order was "lawless" and thus not within the legislative restriction on the reviewing court's jurisdiction. Oestereich v. Selective Service Board, 393 U.S. 233, 89 S.Ct. 414 (1968). In contrast, where a local Board exercises its statutory discretion to determine that an inductee is not a conscientious objector, preinduction review by an injunction proceeding is not available. Clark v. Gabriel, 393 U.S. 256, 89 S.Ct. 424 (1968).

A close examination of these (and other) cases suggests that a host of factors may determine whether administrative action is nonreviewable. These factors include: (1) the precise statutory restriction, if any; (2) the scope of the agency's discretion (a factor which can cut both ways since the broader the discretion the greater need for review); (3) the significance of the individual interest at stake; (4) the comparative expertise and experience of the agency and the court to understand the subject matter; (5) the administrative need for discretion (e.g., speed); and (6) the existence of alternative methods to protect the individual and to prevent abuse of discretion. See, e.g., Hahn v. Gottlieb, 430 F.2d 1243 (1st Cir. 1970).

C. STANDING

Before an administrative decision can be challenged in a court, the person asserting the challenge must have "standing" to seek judicial review. The requirement of standing seeks to serve several functions: to satisfy the "cases" and "controversies" requirement of Article III, § 2 of the Constitution so that the court will have the benefit of a full argument before deciding the matter; to assure that the court's time will not be occupied with frivolous, nuisance suits; and to limit interference with administrative actions to situations where substantial injury is threatened. The basepoint for any discussion of standing is that a named party to an administrative proceeding invariably has standing to seek judicial review. Of course, nonreviewability may prevent review, but there is no question of standing.

The early view was that a person seeking judicial scrutiny of agency action had to show that he had a recognized (by statute or common law), legally protected interest that was adversely affected by the agency's decision. He had to show something more than an adverse personal or economic interest; he had to show a legal right which was invaded. E.g., Alabama Power Co. v. Ickes, 302 U.S. 464, 58 S.Ct. 300 (1938); Tennessee Elec. Power Co. v. TVA, 306 U.S. 118, 59

S.Ct. 366 (1939); see Joint Anti-Fascist Refugee Comm. v. McGrath, 341 U.S. 123, 151–52, 71 S. Ct. 624, 637–38 (1951) (Frankfurter, J., concurring). The circularity of the "legal interest" test (the decision to grant standing is a determination that a legal right has been invaded), its determination only by a preliminary review of the merits (injury plus illegality equals standing) and its rigidity (it depends more on ancient common law concepts of "legal interest" than current notions of the need for a judicial check on a growing federal bureaucracy) led to a crumbling of the doctrinal barriers in the 1940's.

The first major breakthrough occurred in FCC v. Sanders Bros. Radio Station, 309 U.S. 470, 60 S.Ct. 693 (1940). The Court held that the statutory language granting judicial review to "persons aggrieved" by an FCC license decision included not only disappointed applicants but also competitors facing potential economic injury from the agency's action. The test of an "aggrieved person," in other words, was not limited to the assertion of a personal legal wrong. The Court's rationale is significant. It concluded that Congress "may have been of the opinion that one likely to be financially injured by the issue of a license would be the only person having a sufficient interest to bring to the attention of the appellate court errors of law in the action of the

Commission . . . ." This rationale was expanded upon in Scripps-Howard Radio, Inc. v. FCC, 316 U.S. 4, 62 S.Ct. 875 (1942), where the Court pointed out that "these private litigants have standing only as representatives of the public interest." They are, to use Judge Frank's classic phrase, "private Attorney Generals." Associated Indus. v. Ickes, 134 F.2d 694, 704 (2d Cir.), vacated as moot, 320 U.S. 707, 64 S.Ct. 74 (1943). Thus, a complainant was required to demonstrate only *some personal injury* in order to assert the public interest in those situations where statutory provisions for review could be broadly construed. In subsequent years, the Communication Act's review provisions have been read as extending standing to challenge license renewals to peripheral interests, including a manufacturer of consumer electronic products and individuals or groups of listeners. Similar expansions have occurred under other statutory review provisions.

The adoption of the APA in 1946, providing in section 10(a) that a person "adversely affected or aggrieved by agency action within the meaning of a relevant statute" could obtain judicial review (5 U.S.C.A. § 702) eventually contributed to the liberalizing trend. Its main thrust has been to limit administrative power by providing a minimum standard of review in the absence of an express review provision in the relevant statute. In addition, it has also been argued that the Act did not merely codify the existing "legal interest" theory but also expanded the availability of standing by requiring that the complainant prove only that he was adversely affected in fact.* Under this construction of the APA, the *Sanders'* rationale (allowing anyone injured in fact to have standing on behalf of the public interest) would support standing for the plaintiff in all appeals from federal administrative action except when that action is committed to agency discretion or a statute otherwise precludes judicial review.

This construction was not accepted by most courts, however. They concluded that section 10 was merely declaratory of prior law and granted no new rights of judicial review. See, e. g., Arnold Tours, Inc. v. Camp, 408 F.2d 1147, 1151 (1st Cir. 1969), vacated 397 U.S. 315, 90 S.Ct. 1109 (1970); Kansas City Power & Light Co. v. McKay, 225 F.2d 924, 931–32 (D.C. Cir.), cert. denied 350 U.S. 884, 76 S.Ct. 137 (1955). Contra, e. g., Scanwell Laboratories, Inc. v. Shaffer, 424 F.2d 859, 872 (D.C. Cir. 1970). But a number of

* The argument depends on a strained reading of an ambiguous legislative history and an ungrammatical interpretation of the statute. For example, it asserts that the phrase "within the meaning of the relevant statute" modifies only "aggrieved" and not "affected."

lower courts did rely upon section 10 of the APA to allow standing where another statute protects or regulates some interest of the plaintiff's, even though that "relevant statute" did not itself grant judicial review. See, e. g., Road Review League v. Boyd, 270 F.Supp. 650, 660–61 (S.D.N.Y. 1967); Norwalk CORE v. Norwalk Redevelopment Agency, 395 F.2d 920, 933 n. 26 (2d Cir. 1968). In other words, under this view the APA grants standing where the interest asserted by the plaintiff is one Congress has otherwise recognized.

At first the Supreme Court merely did not discourage this trend. In Hardin v. Kentucky Utilities Co., 390 U.S. 1, 88 S.Ct. 651 (1968), the Court held that "when the particular statutory provision invoked does reflect a legislative purpose to protect a competitive interest, the injured competitor has standing to require compliance with that provision." This holding was itself neither new nor novel, the Court having long recognized a statutory interest as a basis for standing, but it was noteworthy that the Court probed the legislative history to find a primary congressional purpose to benefit the plaintiff. Even more significant, in retrospect, was the Court's readiness to distinguish *Kansas City Power & Light Co.,* supra (which had ruled that the APA did not confer standing);

this suggested that the Court might no longer read section 10 so narrowly.*

Then in 1970 the Supreme Court rewrote the law of standing to seek judicial review of administrative action in Association of Data Processing Service Organizations v. Camp, 397 U.S. 150, 90 S.Ct. 827 (1970), and Barlow v. Collins, 397 U.S. 159, 90 S.Ct. 832 (1970). In these companion cases the Court reduced the law of standing to two seemingly straight-forward questions: (1) Is the complainant "aggrieved in fact"; and (2) Is the interest sought to be protected by the complainant "arguably within the zone of interests to be protected or regulated by the statute or constitutional guarantee in question?"

The first requirement of injury in fact seems to be nothing more than an acknowledgement of Article III's constitutional limitation on the judi-

---

* In the same term the Court also held that satisfaction of the case and controversy requirement of Article III— that is, a showing of such a personal stake in the controversy as to assure a "concrete adverseness"—may be all that is necessary to establish standing. In Flast v. Cohen, 392 U.S. 83, 88 S.Ct. 1942 (1968), a taxpayer was allowed to challenge the constitutionality of federal financial aid to parochial schools. Since the taxpayer also had to show a "logical nexus" between his status as a taxpayer and a specific limitation on the congressional taxing and spending power in the Constitution, it is not clear whether injury in fact is the only "constitutional" minimum. In any case, this "minimum" approach generally has not been adopted for determining whether the complainant has standing to seek review of agency action.

cial power of the federal courts. It is satisfied by an allegation that "the challenged action has caused him [the complainant] injury in fact, economic or otherwise." Most courts have found this test easily satisfied, even by groups with only a continuing interest in the environment. But see Sierra Club v. Hickel, 433 F.2d 24 (9th Cir. 1970), cert. granted, 401 U.S. 907, 91 S.Ct. 870 (1971). Two Justices, Brennan and White, would have limited judicial requirements of standing at this point. They assert that the second test goes into the merits and is, in fact, another attempt to consider the reviewability of the case.

The second half of the Court's test—that plaintiff's interest is "arguably within the zone of interests to be protected or regulated by the statute"—is based on section 10 of the APA. No longer must a plaintiff show that the interest he asserts is protected by the statute granting review. Indeed, this test is more relaxed than either section 10 or the lower court cases (such as *Road Review*, supra) because the "relevant statute" need only "arguably" protect plaintiff's interest. The meaning of this test is less clear. It is bound by such elastic terms as "arguably" and "zone," apparently vesting broad discretion in the courts to determine whether standing should be conferred on a particular complainant. It is not clear, for example, whether the focus is on the "interests" asserted or the "persons" asserting the interests. In other words, when challenging the location of a new Disneyland ski resort in a national forest, must the Sierra Club show that *it* is the beneficiary of the act establishing the national forest, or only that the *environmental interest* it asserts is to be protected by the act? Alternatively, is the Sierra Club's own environmental interest as a user of the national forest a sufficient interest, or must its suit claim to protect a broader environmental concern? While these and other questions must await further clarification, it seems clear that the requirements of standing are no longer stringent. Additional pronouncements by the Supreme Court seem likely in the near future. See Sierra Club v. Hickel, supra.

D. EXHAUSTION AND RIPENESS

After *Abbott Laboratories, Data Processing* and *Barlow,* a demand for judicial review of agency action presumably will be granted unless statutorily precluded. Judicial discretion to review agency action is now limited primarily to the timing and context of review. Once reviewability of the subject matter and standing to seek judicial review are determined in favor of the plaintiff, the court may still have to decide at what point a challenger is "adversely affected or aggrieved within the meaning of a relevant statute." The agency's order may still be subject to revision and thus not a "final" order worthy of review. The challenger may have another avenue of administrative relief available and thus not have "exhausted" his administrative remedies. Moreover, the question posed for judicial review may be more suitably considered in another context (e.g., the concrete facts on enforcement) and therefore not "ripe" for judicial review.

Questions of finality, exhaustion, and ripeness are different sides of a similar problem. Finality and exhaustion focus on whether the administrative position being challenged has crystallized and is, in fact, an institutional decision. In other words, what is the effect of review on the administrative process? Ripeness, in contrast, asks whether the issues presented are appropriate for judicial resolution at this time. What is the effect on the court and the challenger if pre-enforcement review is withheld? While each doctrine has a separate and distinct aim, they frequently overlap.

It should be noted, however, that questions of exhaustion or ripeness—as well as questions of reviewability and standing—do not arise when a respondent appeals from an adverse final order or when the agency seeks to enforce its order in court. Exhaustion and ripeness reflect concern with premature review and its effect on the agencies and the courts. The ultimate question is whether the immediate harm caused to the complainant by the administrative "order" outweighs the advantage of allowing the agency to consider the problem more fully or the disadvantage to the court of having to consider issues which might otherwise become moot or more sharply defined. Not surprisingly, the answer depends on the particular circumstances.

In determining whether the challenger should exhaust alternative administrative remedies, the court must first consider the legislative command. For example, Congress entrusted factfinding responsibility and initial decision making under the labor acts to the NLRB. Consequently, a party charged with an unfair labor practice generally cannot challenge the Board's jurisdiction over his activities until the NLRB's adjudicatory process results in a final order. Myers v. Bethlehem Shipbuilding Corp., 303 U.S. 41, 58 S.Ct. 459 (1938).

Nevertheless, the doctrine of exhaustion of administrative remedies is not carried beyond practical bounds. For example, a draft registrant seeking to challenge his classification must usually first appeal to a superior board within the selective service system. However, an orphan seeking exemption as a "sole surviving son" may challenge the validity of his classification (and the induction order) when criminally prosecuted for refusing to submit to induction even though he failed to exercise his right to appeal within the administrative system. McKart v. United States, 395 U.S. 185, 89 S.Ct. 1657 (1969). Although the time for administrative appeal was past (and the administrative process was therefore not being prematurely interrupted), judicial review in the *McKart* situation usually runs counter to the purpose of the exhaustion doctrine because it allows draft registrants to avoid the administrative process seemingly in opposition to the legislative command. In allowing judicial review, the Court relied upon several factors: (1) significant harm was alleged by the challenger (a prison sentence); (2) the issue had crystallized and seemed appropriate for judicial resolution (no additional facts were needed; the question involved statutory interpretation rather than administrative discretion or expertise); (3) the error was serious (plain error of law); (4) administrative relief seemed unavailable and futile (the time for further administrative review had passed; the national headquarters had already rejected similar claims); (5) the interference with the agency's operation was minimal (there was no interruption).

Although the doctrine of ripeness for judicial review is not unrelated to the policy behind Article III of the Constitution, which requires concrete controversies, that command is satisfied by the first requirement of standing (injury in fact). The basic rationale of ripeness, as the Supreme Court explained in the leading case of Abbott Laboratories v. Gardner, 387 U.S. 136, 148–49, 87 S.Ct. 1507, 1515 (1967), "is to prevent the courts, through avoidance of premature adjudication, from entangling themselves in abstract disagreements over administrative policies, and also to protect the agencies from judicial interference until an administrative decision has been formalized and its effects felt in a concrete way by the challenging parties. The problem is best seen in a twofold aspect, requiring us to *evaluate both the fitness of the issues for judicial decision and the hardship to the parties of withholding court consideration.*" (Emphasis added.)

In *Abbott Laboratories* the Court held that an FDA regulation was ripe for judicial consideration at the request of 37 drug manufacturers (who accounted for over 90% of all drugs sold) and their trade association. The Food and Drug Act requires, inter alia, that a prescription drug's generic ("established") name be printed "prominently" on all drug labeling. In implementing this provision, FDA regula-

tions would have required that the generic
name appear every time the trade ("proprietary") name was used. The court upheld pre-
enforcement review over the FDA's objection
that a judicial test should await agency prosecution for failure to comply with the regulation.
Several factors were controlling: the issue was
purely legal (what did the statutory term "prominently" encompass?); withholding review
would be costly and potentially very harmful to
the challengers (they faced the choice between
spending millions in compliance or being brand-
ed criminal violators with attendant publicity and
fines); judicial efficiency was improved by immediate review (a multiplicity of enforcement
suits could thereby be avoided); and administrative reconsiderations of the rule seemed unlikely
(it was issued after notice-and-comment hearings). The basic point is that in these circumstances it would have been unfair to require the
drug companies to incur the risks of criminal
sanctions and adverse public reaction in order to
test the legality of administrative action.

A companion case, Toilet Goods Ass'n v. Gardner, 387 U.S. 158, 87 S.Ct. 1520 (1967), illustrates an application of the ripeness doctrine to
postpone review. The Food and Drug Act pro-
hibits the use in cosmetics (as well as in foods or
drugs) of colors from batches that have not been

certified. The FDA adopted regulations stating that its certification service would be foreclosed to a manufacturer if they denied FDA inspectors "free access" to manufacturing processes and color additive formulas. A suit to challenge the validity of a regulation before the agency sought enforcement was "not appropriate for judicial resolution," even though the agency had taken final action and the issue involved a purely legal question. Several factors were significant. The contours of permissible access regulations depended upon the need for supervision, specific enforcement problems, and the agency's internal safeguards to protect trade secrets. Resolution of these issues appeared to depend upon facts developed in an enforcement context. In addition, no hardship was immediately imposed upon the challengers since the regulation would have no impact until access was sought and refused.

CHAPTER XII

SCOPE OF JUDICIAL REVIEW

Without judicial review, administrative action and discretion would be limited only by agency self-discipline, executive direction, or legislative and public pressure. Such controls are, at best, limitations on gross abuses of authority. Because they are addressed to administrative action generally, their impact on routine cases or specific actions is likely to be minimal. In contrast, judicial review operates on a single case or rule basis and addresses itself to individual administrative decisions. It considers the authority and legitimacy of an order or rule rather than the overall performance of the administrator or agency. Even then, of course, the scope of the rule is restricted because the court examines only whether the administrator acted within his delegated authority and did not abuse his discretion, *not* whether he acted wisely or correctly. This discussion, therefore, focuses on the extent to which the reviewing court will defer to the administrative agency's judgment.

Judicial review is available to test whether the agency has acted ultra vires by exceeding its constitutional or statutory authority, has interpreted and applied relevant statutes correctly, has understood and evaluated the evidence reasonably, and has conducted a fair proceeding in accordance with the agency's rules. Although almost any aspect of the administrative operation may be subjected to judicial scrutiny, the over-riding (or at least most significant) factor is that the agency is the body delegated with responsibility for carrying out the legislative program. It has the experience and sometimes the expertise. Hence, where possible, courts reviewing administrative action generally defer to the agency's determination if it has a reasonable basis.

The general principle of judicial deference has been translated into several rules to guide judicial review of administrative action. First, an agency's findings of "fact"—basic or raw facts—will be upheld if supported by substantial evidence on the whole record. Second, inferences or ultimate fact findings will withstand judicial scrutiny if they have a "rational basis." Finally, only questions of law—the agency's authority, the meaning of a statutory term, its application to the facts, procedural requirements—are reviewed de novo; a court is theoretically free to determine for itself the correctness of the agency's legal judgments. However, even then the agency's interpretations are often entitled to great weight.

These rules are subject to considerable qualification and in some cases even the concepts they seek to embody are questioned. Nevertheless, the initial difficulty lies in their meaning and application. There is surprisingly little agreement on how questions of fact and law can be distinguished. Definitions tend to obscure rather than to clarify. The basic distinction is that an agency's fact findings are not dependent upon any assertion of their legal effect. For example, a finding by a workmen's compensation commission that an employee while at work was intentionally hit on the head by another employee is a finding of fact. The agency's view of the compensation statute is not related to this finding. It determines, rather, what happened, to whom, where, when and how. A determination that his injury arose out of his employment relation and is therefore compensable is a conclusion of law. It requires knowledge and an application of the compensation statute. However, seldom is the distinction so readily drawn. And it is not uncommon for members of a reviewing court to disagree with each other on whether the issue is one of fact requiring deference or one of law calling for closer judicial scrutiny. This suggests, of course, that other factors such as the agency's experience and expertness may in fact determine the standard of judicial review.

A. QUESTIONS OF FACT

In most cases, the standard for review of an agency's findings of fact is whether the agency's determination is "supported by substantial evidence on the record considered as a whole." A court reviewing fact determinations is generally limited to a veto of the agency's findings. Only the agency is delegated authority to make positive findings.

Other tests are possible. It could be argued (and some critics still do) that administrative arbitrariness will be checked only by broad judicial review of fact determinations. They propose that administrative findings be reviewed under the same standard as a judge sitting without a jury—the "clearly erroneous" test—where the reviewing court may reverse when it takes a contrary view of the evidence even though there is evidence to support the finding. The opposite view is suggested by others seeking to avoid judicial interference with administrative programs. Under this narrower standard of review, the agency's findings should be accepted when supported by any record evidence. The substantial evidence standard is a compromise between these positions. It upholds agency determinations of fact if a "reasoning" mind could make the same finding; under it the court does not defer to the agency merely because there is record evidence supporting the finding.

The substantial evidence test is now firmly entrenched in most agency enabling statutes and in section 10(e) of the APA (5 U.S.C.A. § 706). It is defined as "more than a mere scintilla. It means such relevant evidence as a reasonable mind might accept as adequate to support a conclusion. . . . [This] does not go so far as to justify orders without a basis in evidence having rational probative force." Consolidated Edison Co. v. NLRB, 305 U.S. 197, 59 S.Ct. 206 (1938). The supporting evidence must be of the kind upon which responsible persons are accustomed to rely; this may include—and even be limited to—hearsay. See Richardson v. Perales, 402 U.S. 389, 91 S.Ct. 1420 (1971). It must be enough to justify a refusal to direct a verdict if the trial were to a jury; yet it is less than the weight (or preponderance) of the evidence, and the fact that the record also supports inconsistent conclusions does not mean that the agency's findings are inadequately supported. NLRB v. Columbian Enameling & Stamping Co., 306 U.S. 292, 59 S.Ct. 501 (1939); NLRB v. Nevada Consolidated Copper Corp., 316 U.S. 105, 62 S.Ct. 960 (1942). In the last analysis, the amount of record evidence which constitutes substantial evidence is left to the review court's sound discretion.

Although the substantial evidence rule allows a reviewing court wide latitude, in practice the courts do not second guess most agency findings. The rationale for this approach was recently summarized by the Court in Consolo v. FMC, 383 U.S. 607, 86 S.Ct. 1018 (1966): "Congress was very deliberate in adopting this standard of review. It frees the reviewing courts of the time-consuming and difficult task of weighing the evidence, it gives proper respect to the expertise of the administrative tribunal and it helps promote the uniform application of the statute."

At one time it was unclear whether an administrative finding would be upheld so long as there was some substantial evidence in the record. That is, was the court's task on review completed when, after examining those portions of the record which supported the finding, it determined that the evidence was "substantial"? In the leading case of Universal Camera Corp. v. NLRB, 340 U.S. 474, 71 S.Ct. 456 (1951), the Court answered the question: "The substantiality of evidence must take into account whatever in the record fairly detracts from its weight." Before accepting the agency's finding, the review court must consider the contradictory evidence, if any, in the record which is cited to the court; then it determines whether the agency's finding is reasonable.

Of course the record may not contain the most important evidence relied upon by the trial examiner and the agency in making findings of fact. The witness' demeanor may determine the weight given his testimony. The cold record on review—usually the verbatim transcript, the pleadings, and the rulings by the examiner and the agency—may not be the equivalent of seeing the witness and hearing his testimony. Consequently, where the agency's findings of fact are based upon the examiner's evaluation of the witness' credibility and that credibility depends (at least in part) on the witness' demeanor, such findings are entitled to relatively greater weight in determining whether the substantial evidence test is met. Similar deference is paid to agency findings within the special competence of the agency.

Despite general agreement today on the semantic meaning of the substantial evidence test, its application continues to be disputed. The reasons are several. First, the test itself allows the courts a wide opportunity for choice and self-restraint. Second, evidence cannot be measured objectively. What is sufficient is a matter of opinion and requires the exercise of judgment where differences are not uncommon. Third, courts are influenced undoubtedly by a variety of other, inarticulate factors: "The character of the administrative agency, the nature of the problems with which it deals, the nature and consequences of the administrative action, the confidence which the agency has won, the degree to which the review would interfere with the agency's functions or burden the courts, the nature of the proceedings before the administrative agency, and similar factors." Attorney General's Report on Administrative Procedure in Government Agencies 91, S. Doc. No. 8, 77th Cong. 1st Sess. 91 (1941).

B.   QUESTIONS OF LAW

Similar uncertainty surrounds the scope of judicial review of an agency's conclusions of law. Not only do these same "inarticulate factors" apply, but also it is invariably disputed whether the issue involves a question of fact, law or mixed law-and-fact—and, consequently, the appropriate standard for judicial review is challenged. Once this issue is passed, the general rule is that the "reviewing court shall decide all relevant questions of law, interpret constitutional and statutory provisions, and determine the meaning or applicability of the terms of an agency action." 5 U.S.C.A. § 706.

Questions of law where the reviewing court may substitute its own judgment or make its own evaluation—that is, where the scope of review may be unlimited—cover several distinct issues. First, the determination of whether the agency violated a constitutional mandate is a question of law. Courts, not agencies, are the final interpreters of governmental powers in our constitutional framework; they are the delegated experts. Marbury v. Madison, 5 U.S. (1 Cranch) 137 (1803); see Cooper v. Aaron, 358 U.S. 1, 18–19, 78 S.Ct. 1401, 1409–10 (1958). Second, the court determines whether the agency acted ultra vires. That is, the question of whether the agency strayed from the delegated path assigned to it by the legislature is subject to independent judicial determination. The reviewing court ascertains the legislative intention and whether administrative action is consistent with it. Third, the courts are the final arbiters of what factors or standards should be applied by the administrator. For example, an agency may be authorized to issue a hydroelectric plant construction permit in accordance with the public interest, convenience and necessity. Whether the aesthetic, conservational and recreational impact of such a license should be considered under the statutory mandate is ultimately a question for the court. However, the judicial determination of the appropriate agency standard should be distinguished from the agency's task of applying these criteria —which is usually tested on review by whether the agency's determination has a rational basis.

For example, once the reviewing court is satisfied that the agency appropriately took these "environmental" factors into account in deciding whether to issue the construction permit, the court's review of the agency decision will be limited to whether its decision is supported by substantial evidence and has a reasonable basis.

Thus, whether the court will give unlimited or only a limited review to the agency's determination depends primarily upon the precise issue before the court and the legislative intention. A review of the two leading cases illustrates judicial reliance on this functional approach.

In Gray v. Powell, 314 U.S. 402, 62 S.Ct. 326 (1941), the Supreme Court upheld the administrator's application of the statutory term "producer" to deny a coal-burning railroad its requested exemption from marketing restrictions under the Bituminous Coal Act. The Court's review was both unlimited and limited. It gave unlimited review to whether the statute's price control provisions covered coal deliveries involving no change in ownership (the railroad argued that it was exempt as a self-consumer from its own mines). The Court determined for itself, without relying upon the administrator's conclusions, that a change in the coal's ownership was not required for a firm to be found to be a producer within the coverage of the Act. In addition, the Court independently determined that Congress had given the administrator discretion to exempt companies that produced coal for their own consumption from the Act *if* exemption would not adversely affect the regulated scheme. Here the administrator had discretion and the Court would not substitute its judgment as long as the administrator applied the correct factors. Since the administrator applied the appropriate criteria —the impact of exemption on the regulatory program—his determination was upheld under a test of limited review.

Similar review criteria were applied in NLRB v. Hearst, 322 U.S. 111, 64 S.Ct. 851 (1944). The ultimate question was whether the term "employees" in the National Labor Relations Act applied to newsboys. The newspaper argued that its street vendors were not employees covered by the Act, relying upon common law and state law rulings that the newsboys met the legal criteria for independent contractors. The agency contended, instead, that the newsboys were under the Board's jurisdiction because the Act was designed to protect such persons and the Act's remedies were appropriate. In upholding the Board, the Court independently determined that neither state nor common law definitions applied and that the criteria applied by the Board for determining whether newsboys were employees of the newspaper were correct. Then, satisfied that the Board had correctly read its statutory mandate and that particular applications were within the Board's discretion, the Court relied upon only a limited review to assure itself that the agency had properly applied these criteria to the newspaper and its newsboys here. In other words, the scope of review of "questions of law" depends upon the judicial function.

However, it must be acknowledged that all cases (even all Supreme Court cases) simply will not parse, and that courts do not always apply this functional analysis. The comparative qualifications of the court and agency to decide a particular question appear particularly significant. And in some cases, particularly decisions reviewing workmen's compensation awards, administrative expertise or judicial deference to the administrator's judgment seems controlling. See, e. g., O'Keeffe v. Smith, Hinchman, Grylls, Assoc., 380 U.S. 359, 85 S.Ct. 1012 (1965).

•

APPENDIX

ADMINISTRATIVE PROCEDURE ACT

UNITED STATES CODE

TITLE 5—GOVERNMENT ORGANIZATION AND EMPLOYEES

PART I—THE AGENCIES GENERALLY

* * *

CHAPTER 5—ADMINISTRATIVE PROCEDURE

* * *

Subchapter II—Administrative Procedure

**Parallel
sections of
1946 Act**

§ 551. Definitions

For the purpose of this subchapter—

(1) "agency" means each authority of the Government of the United States, whether or not it is within or subject to review by another agency, but does not include—

(A) the Congress;

(B) the courts of the United States;

Sec. 2(a).

(C) the governments of the territories or possessions of the United States;

(D) the government of the District of Columbia;
or except as to the requirements of section 552 of this title—

(E) agencies composed of representatives of the parties or of representatives of organizations of the parties to the disputes determined by them;

(F) courts martial and military commissions;

(G) military authority exercised in the field in time of war or in occupied territory; or

(H) functions conferred by sections 1738, 1739, 1743, and 1744 of title 12; chapter 2 of title 41; or sections 1622, 1884, 1891–1902, and former section 1641(b) (2), of title 50, appendix;

(2) "person" includes an individual, partnership, corporation, association, or public or private organization other than an agency;   Sec. 2(b).

(3) "party" includes a person or agency named or admitted as a party, or property seeking and entitled as of

right to be admitted as a party, in an
agency proceeding, and a person or
agency admitted by an agency as a
party for limited purposes;

(4) "rule" means the whole or a
part of an agency statement of general or particular applicability and future effect designed to implement, interpret, or prescribe law or policy or
describing the organization, procedure,
or practice requirements of an agency
and includes the approval or prescription for the future of rates, wages,
corporate or financial structures or reorganization thereof, prices, facilities,
appliances, services or allowances therefor or of valuations, costs, or account-
ing, or practices bearing on any of the
foregoing;

(5) "rule making" means agency
process for formulating, amending, or
repealing a rule;

(6) "order" means the whole or a
part of a final disposition, whether affirmative, negative, injunctive, or declaratory in form, of an agency in a
matter other than rule making but including licensing;

(7) "adjudication" means agency
process for the formulation of an order;

SEC. 2(c).

SEC. 2(d).

**Parallel
sections of
1946 Act**

(8) "license" includes the whole or a part of an agency permit, certificate, approval, registration, charter, membership, statutory exemption or other form of permission; SEC. 2(e).

(9) "licensing" includes agency process respecting the grant, renewal, denial, revocation, suspension, annulment, withdrawal, limitation, amendment, modification, or conditioning of a license;

(10) "sanction" includes the whole or a part of an agency— SEC. 2(f).

(A) prohibition, requirement, limitation, or other condition affecting the freedom of a person;

(B) withholding of relief;

(C) imposition of penalty or fine;

(D) destruction, taking, seizure, or withholding of property;

(E) assessment of damages, reimbursement, restitution, compensation, costs, charges, or fees;

(F) requirement, revocation, or suspension of a license; or

(G) taking other compulsory or restrictive action;

(11) "relief" includes the whole or a part of an agency—

(A) grant of money, assistance, license, authority, exemption, exception, privilege, or remedy;

(B) recognition of a claim, right, immunity, privilege, exemption, or exception; or

(C) taking of other action on the application or petition of, and beneficial to, a person;

(12) "agency proceeding" means an agency process as defined by paragraphs (5), (7), and (9) of this section; and   Sec. 2(g).

(13) "agency action" includes the whole or a part of an agency rule, order, license, sanction, relief, or the equivalent or denial thereof, or failure to act.

§ 552. Public information; agency rules, opinions, orders, records, and proceedings   Sec. 3. (as amended)

(a) Each agency shall make available to the public information as follows:

(1) Each agency shall separately state and currently publish in the Federal Register for the guidance of the public—   Sec. 3(a)

(A) descriptions of its central and field organization and the established places at which, the employees (and in the case of a uniformed service, the members) from whom, and the methods whereby, the public may obtain information, make submittals or requests, or obtain decisions;

(B) statements of the general course and method by which its functions are channeled and determined, including the nature and requirements of all formal and informal procedures available;

(C) rules of procedure, descriptions of forms available or the places at which forms may be obtained, and instructions as to the scope and contents of all papers, reports, or examinations;

(D) substantive rules of general applicability adopted as authorized by law, and statements of general policy or interpretations of general applicability formulated and adopted by the agency; and

(E) each amendment, revision, or repeal of the foregoing.

Except to the extent that a person has actual and timely notice of the terms thereof, a person may not in any manner be required to resort to, or be adversely affected by, a matter required to be published in the Federal Register and not so published. For the purpose of this paragraph, matter reasonably available to the class of persons affected thereby is deemed published in the Federal Register when incorporated by reference therein with the approval of the Director of the Federal Register.

(2) Each agency, in accordance with published rules, shall make available for public inspection and copying— SEC. 3(b).

(A) final opinions, including concurring and dissenting opinions, as well as orders, made in the adjudication of cases;

(B) those statements of policy and interpretations which have been adopted by the agency and are not published in the Federal Register; and

(C) administrative staff manuals and instructions to staff that affect a member of the public;

unless the materials are promptly published and copies offered for sale. To the extent required to prevent a clearly unwarranted invasion of personal privacy, an agency may delete identifying details when it makes available or publishes an opinion, statement of policy, interpretation, or staff manual or instruction. However, in each case the justification for the deletion shall be explained fully in writing. Each agency also shall maintain and make available for public inspection and copying a current index providing identifying information for the public as to any matter issued, adopted, or promulgated after July 4, 1967, and required by this paragraph to be made available or published. A final order, opinion, statement of policy, interpretation, or staff manual or instruction that affects a member of the public may be relied on, used, or cited as precedent by an agency against a party other than an agency only if—

(i) it has been indexed and either made available or published as provided by this paragraph; or

(ii) the party has actual and timely notice of the terms thereof.

(3) Except with respect to the records made available under paragraphs (1) and (2) of this subsection, each agency, on request for identifiable records, made in accordance with publish-

SEC. 3(c).

[*283*]

ed rules stating the time, place, fees
to the extent authorized by statute, and
procedure to be followed, shall make
the records promptly available to any
person. On complaint, the district
court of the United States in the district in which the complainant resides,
or has his principal place of business,
or in which the agency records are situated, has jurisdiction to enjoin the
agency from withholding agency records and to order the production of
any agency records improperly withheld
from the complainant. In such a case
the court shall determine the matter de
novo and the burden is on the agency
to sustain its action. In the event of
noncompliance with the order of the
court, the district court may punish for
contempt the responsible employee, and
in the case of a uniformed service, the
responsible member. Except as to
causes the court considers of greater
importance, proceedings before the district court, as authorized by this paragraph, take precedence on the docket
over all other causes and shall be assigned for hearing and trial at the
earliest practicable date and expedited
in every way.

(4) Each agency having more than
one member shall maintain and make

available for public inspection a record of the final votes of each member in every agency proceeding.

(b) This section does not apply to matters that are—

(1) specifically required by Executive order to be kept secret in the interest of the national defense or foreign policy;

(2) related solely to the internal personnel rules and practices of an agency;

(3) specifically exempted from disclosure by statute;

(4) trade secrets and commercial or financial information obtained from a person and privileged or confidential;

(5) inter-agency or intra-agency memorandums or letters which would not be available by law to a party other than an agency in litigation with the agency;

(6) personnel and medical files and similar files the disclosure of which would constitute a clearly unwarranted invasion of personal privacy;

(7) investigatory files compiled for law enforcement purposes except

APPENDIX

to the extent available by law to a
party other than an agency;

(8) contained in or related to examination, operating, or condition reports prepared by, on behalf of, or
for the use of an agency responsible
for the regulation or supervision of
financial institutions; or

(9) geological and geophysical information and data, including maps,
concerning wells.

(c) This section does not authorize
withholding of information or limit the
availability of records to the public,
except as specifically stated in this section.   This section is not authority to
withhold information from Congress.

§ 553. **Rule making**   SEC. 4.

(a) This section applies, accordingly to the provisions thereof, except to
the extent that there is involved—

(1) a military or foreign affairs
function of the United States; or

(2) a matter relating to agency
management or personnel or to public property, loans, grants, benefits,
or contracts.

(b) General notice of proposed rule   SEC. 4(a).
making shall be published in the Federal Register, unless persons subject

[*286*]

**Parallel
sections of
1946 Act**

thereto are named and either personally served or otherwise have actual notice thereof in accordance with law. The notice shall include—

(1) a statement of the time, place, and nature of public rule making proceedings;

(2) reference to the legal authority under which the rule is proposed; and

(3) either the terms or substance of the proposed rule or a description of the subjects and issues involved.

Except when notice or hearing is required by statute, this subsection does not apply—

(A) to interpretative rules, general statements of policy, or rules of agency organization, procedure, or practice; or

(B) when the agency for good cause finds (and incorporates the finding and a brief statement of reasons therefor in the rules issued) that notice and public procedure thereon are impracticable, unnecessary, or contrary to the public interest.

(c) After notice required by this sec-SEC. 4(**b**). tion, the agency shall give interested persons an opportunity to participate in the rule making through submission of written data, views, or arguments with or without opportunity for oral presentation. After consideration of the relevant matter presented, the agency shall incorporate in the rules adopted a concise general statement of their basis and purpose. When rules are required by statute to be made on the record after opportunity for an agency hearing, sections 556 and 557 of this title apply instead of this subsection.

(d) The required publication or service of a substantive rule shall be made not less than 30 days before its effective date, except—

Sec. 4(c).

(1) a substantive rule which grants or recognizes an exemption or relieves a restriction;

(2) interpretative rules and statements of policy; or

(3) as otherwise provided by the agency for good cause found and published with the rule.

(e) Each agency shall give an interested person the right to petition for the issuance, amendment, or repeal of a rule.

Sec. 4(d).

§ 554. Adjudications

(a) This section applies, according to the provisions thereof, in every case of adjudication required by statute to be determined on the record after opportunity for an agency hearing, except to the extent that there is involved—

(1) a matter subject to a subsequent trial of the law and the facts de novo in a court;

(2) the selection or tenure of an employee, except a hearing examiner appointed under section 3105 of this title;

(3) proceedings in which decisions rest solely on inspections, tests, or elections;

(4) the conduct of military or foreign affairs functions;

(5) cases in which an agency is acting as an agent for a court; or

(6) the certification of worker representatives.

(b) Persons entitled to notice of an agency hearing shall be timely informed of— SEC. 5(a).

(1) the time, place, and nature of the hearing;

[*289*]

(2) the legal authority and jurisdiction under which the hearing is to be held; and

(3) the matters of fact and law asserted.

When private persons are the moving parties, other parties to the proceeding shall give prompt notice of issues controverted in fact or law; and in other instances agencies may by rule require responsive pleading. In fixing the time and place for hearings, due regard shall be had for the convenience and necessity of the parties or their representatives.

(c) The agency shall give all interested parties opportunity for— Sec. 5(b).

(1) the submission and consideration of facts, arguments, offers of settlement, or proposals of adjustment when time, the nature of the proceeding, and the public interest permit; and

(2) to the extent that the parties are unable so to determine a controversy by consent, hearing and decision on notice and in accordance with sections 556 and 557 of this title.

(d) The employee who presides at Sec. 5(c).
the reception of evidence pursuant to

[*290*]

section 556 of this title shall make the
recommended decision or initial decision required by section 557 of this
title, unless he becomes unavailable to
the agency. Except to the extent required for the disposition of ex parte
matters as authorized by law, such an
employee may not—

(1) consult a person or party on a
fact in issue, unless on notice and
opportunity for all parties to participate; or

(2) be responsible to or subject
to the supervision or direction of an
employee or agent engaged in the
performance of investigative or
prosecuting functions for an agency.

An employee or agent engaged in the
performance of investigative or prosecuting functions for an agency in a
case may not, in that or a factually related case, participate or advise in the
decision, recommended decision, or
agency review pursuant to section 557
of this title, except as witness or counsel in public proceedings. This subsection does not apply—

(A) in determining applications
for initial licenses;

(B) to proceedings involving the
validity or application of rates, facil-

ities, or practices of public utilities
or carriers; or

(C) to the agency or a member or
members of the body comprising the
agency.

(e) The agency, with like effect as
in the case of other orders, and in its
sound discretion, may issue a declaratory order to terminate a controversy
or remove uncertainty.

SEC. 5(d).

§ 555. Ancillary matters

SEC. 6.

(a) This section applies, according
to the provisions thereof, except as
otherwise provided by this subchapter.

(b) A person compelled to appear
in person before an agency or representative thereof is entitled to be accompanied, represented, and advised by
counsel or, if permitted by the agency,
by other qualified representative. A
party is entitled to appear in person or
by or with counsel or other duly qualified representative in an agency proceeding. So far as the orderly conduct of public business permits, an interested person may appear before an
agency or its responsible employees for
the presentation, adjustment, or determination of an issue, request, or controversy in a proceeding, whether inter-

SEC. 6(a).

locutory, summary, or otherwise, or in connection with an agency function. With due regard for the convenience and necessity of the parties or their representatives and within a reasonable time, each agency shall proceed to conclude a matter presented to it. This subsection does not grant or deny a person who is not a lawyer the right to appear for or represent others before an agency or in an agency proceeding.

(c) Process, requirement of a report, inspection, or other investigative act or demand may not be issued, made, or enforced except as authorized by law. A person compelled to submit data or evidence is entitled to retain or, on payment of lawfully prescribed costs, procure a copy or transcript thereof, except that in a nonpublic investigatory proceeding the witness may for good cause be limited to inspection of the official transcript of his testimony.

SEC. 6(b).

(d) Agency subpenas authorized by law shall be issued to a party on request and, when required by rules of procedure, on a statement or showing of general relevance and reasonable scope of the evidence sought. On con-

SEC. 6(c).

test, the court shall sustain the subpena or similar process or demand to the extent that it is found to be in accordance with law. In a proceeding for enforcement, the court shall issue an order requiring the appearance of the witness or the production of the evidence or data within a reasonable time under penalty of punishment for contempt in cases of contumacious failure to comply.

(e) Prompt notice shall be given of the denial in whole or in part of a written application, petition, or other request of an interested person made in connection with any agency proceeding. Except in affirming a prior denial or when the denial is self-explanatory, the notice shall be accompanied by a brief statement of the grounds for denial.

Sec. 6(d).

§ 556. Hearings; presiding employees; powers and duties; burden of proof; evidence; record as basis of decision

Sec. 7.

(a) This section applies, according to the provisions thereof, to hearings required by section 553 or 554 of this title to be conducted in accordance with this section.

**Parallel
sections of
1946 Act**

(b) There shall preside at the tak-   Sec. 7(a).
ing of evidence—

    (1) the agency;

    (2) one or more members of the
body which comprises the agency;
or

    (3) one or more hearing examin-
ers appointed under section 3105 of
this title.

This subchapter does not supersede the
conduct of specified classes of proceedings, in whole or in part, by or before
boards or other employees specially
provided for by or designated under
statute. The functions of presiding
employees and of employees participating in decisions in accordance with section 557 of this title shall be conducted
in an impartial manner. A presiding
or participating employee may at any
time disqualify himself. On the filing
in good faith of a timely and sufficient
affidavit of personal bias or other disqualification of a presiding or participating employee, the agency shall determine the matters as a part of the
record and decision in the case.

(c) Subject to published rules of the   Sec. 7(b).
agency and within its powers, employ-
ees presiding at hearings may—

(1) administer oaths and affirmations;

(2) issue subpenas authorized by law;

(3) rule on offers of proof and receive relevant evidence;

(4) take depositions or have depositions taken when the ends of justice would be served;

(5) regulate the course of the hearing;

(6) hold conferences for the settlement or simplification of the issues by consent of the parties;

(7) dispose of procedural requests or similar matters;

(8) make or recommend decisions in accordance with section 557 of this title; and

(9) take other action authorized by agency rule consistent with this subchapter.

(d) Except as otherwise provided by statute, the proponent of a rule or order has the burden of proof. Any oral or documentary evidence may be received, but the agency as a matter of policy shall provide for the exclusion of irrelevant, immaterial, or unduly repetitious evidence. A sanction may

SEC. 7(c).

not be imposed or rule or order issued **except** on consideration of the whole record or those parts thereof cited by a party and supported by and in accordance with the reliable, probative, and substantial evidence. A party is entitled to present his case or defense by oral or documentary evidence, to submit rebuttal evidence, and to conduct such cross-examination as may be required for a full and true disclosure of the facts. In rule making or determining claims for money or benefits or applications for initial licenses an agency may, when a party will not be prejudiced thereby, adopt procedures for the submission of all or part of the evidence in written form.

(e) The transcript of testimony and exhibits, together with all papers and requests filed in the proceeding, constitutes the exclusive record for decision in accordance with section 557 of this title and, on payment of lawfully prescribed costs, shall be made available to the parties. When an agency decision rests on official notice of a material fact not appearing in the evidence in the record, a party is entitled, on timely request, to an opportunity to show the contrary.

SEC. 7(d).

APPENDIX

§ 557. Initial decisions; conclusive-
   ness; review by agency;
   submissions by parties;
   contents of decisions; record

SEC. 8.

(a) This section applies, according
to the provisions thereof, when a hearing is required to be conducted in accordance with section 556 of this title.

(b) When the agency did not preside at the reception of the evidence,
the presiding employee or, in cases not
subject to section 554(d) of this title,
an employee qualified to preside at
hearings pursuant to section 556 of this
title, shall initially decide the case unless the agency requires, either in specific cases or by general rule, the entire
record to be certified to it for decision.
When the presiding employee makes an
initial decision, that decision then becomes the decision of the agency without further proceedings unless there is
an appeal to, or review on motion of,
the agency within time provided by
rule. On appeal from or review of the
initial decision, the agency has all the
powers which it would have in making
the initial decision except as it may
limit the issues on notice or by rule.
When the agency makes the decision

SEC. 8(a).

without having presided at the reception of the evidence, the presiding employee or an employee qualified to preside at hearings pursuant to section 556 of this title shall first recommend a decision, except that in rule making or determining application for initial licenses—

(1) instead thereof the agency may issue a tentative decision or one of its responsible employees may recommend a decision; or

(2) this procedure may be omitted in a case in which the agency finds on the record that due and timely execution of its functions imperatively and unavoidably so requires.

(c) Before a recommended, initial, or tentative decision, or a decision on agency review of the decision of subordinate employees, the parties are entitled to a reasonable opportunity to submit for the consideration of the employees participating in the decisions—

Sec. 8(b).

(1) proposed findings and conclusions; or

(2) exceptions to the decisions or recommended decisions of subordi-

nate employees or to tentative agency decisions; and

(3) supporting reasons for the exceptions or proposed findings or conclusions.

The record shall show the ruling on each finding, conclusion, or exception presented. All decisions, including initial, recommended, and tentative decisions, are a part of the record and shall include a statement of—

(A) findings and conclusions, and the reasons or basis therefor, on all the material issues of fact, law, or discretion presented on the record; and

(B) the appropriate rule, order, sanction, relief, or denial thereof.

§ 558. **Imposition of sanctions; determination of applications for licenses; suspension, revocation, and expiration of licenses**

Sec. 9.

(a) This section applies, according to the provisions thereof, to the exercise of a power or authority.

(b) A sanction may not be imposed or a substantive rule or order issued except within jurisdiction delegated to the agency and as authorized by law.

Sec. 9(a).

**Parallel
sections of
1946 Act**
Sec. 9(b).

(c) When application is made for a
license required by law, the agency,
with due regard for the rights and
privileges of all the interested parties
or adversely affected persons and
within a reasonable time, shall set and
complete proceedings required to be
conducted in accordance with sections
556 and 557 of this title or other proceedings required by law and shall make
its decision. Except in cases of will-
fulness or those in which public health,
interest, or safety requires otherwise,
the withdrawal, suspension, revocation,
or annulment of a license is lawful only
if, before the institution of agency proceedings therefor, the licensee has been
given—

(1) notice by the agency in writing of the facts or conduct which
may warrant the action; and

(2) opportunity to demonstrate or
achieve compliance with all lawful
requirements.

When the licensee has made timely and
sufficient application for a renewal or
a new license in accordance with agency
rules, a license with reference to an
activity of a continuing nature does
not expire until the application has been
finally determined by the agency.

[*301*]

§ 559. Effect on other laws; effect of subsequent statute

This subchapter, chapter 7, and sections 1305, 3105, 3344, 4301(2) (E), 5362, and 7521, and the provisions of section 5335(a) (B) of this title that relate to hearing examiners, do not limit or repeal additional requirements imposed by statute or otherwise recognized by law. Except as otherwise required by law, requirements or privileges relating to evidence or procedure apply equally to agencies and persons. Each agency is granted the authority necessary to comply with the requirements of this subchapter through the issuance of rules or otherwise. Subsequent statute may not be held to supersede or modify this subchapter, chapter 7, sections 1305, 3105, 3344, 4301 (2) (E), 5362, or 7521, or the provisions of section 5335(a) (B) of this title that relate to hearing examiners, except to the extent that it does so expressly.

* * *

Chapter 7—Judicial Review

**Parallel
sections of
1946 Act**

§ 701. Application; definitions

(a) This chapter applies, according to the provisions thereof, except to the extent that—

Sec. 10.
[Introductory clause].

(1) statutes preclude judicial review; or

(2) agency action is committed to agency discretion by law.

(b) For the purpose of this chapter—*

(1) "agency" means each authority of the Government of the United States, whether or not it is within or subject to review by another agency, but does not include—

Sec. 2(a).

(A) the Congress;

(B) the courts of the United States;

* § 701(b) (1) is identical to § 551(1) (A) through (H).

(C) the governments of the territories or possessions of the United States;

(D) the government of the District of Columbia;

(E) agencies composed of representatives of the parties or of representatives of organizations of the parties to the disputes determined by them;

(F) courts martial and military commissions;

(G) military authority exercised in the field in time of war or in occupied territory; or

(H) functions conferred by sections 1738, 1739, 1743, and 1744 of title 12; chapter 2 of title 41; or sections 1622, 1884, 1891–1902, and former section 1641(b) (2), of title 50, appendix; and

(2) "person", "rule", "order", "license", "sanction", "relief", and "agency action" have the meanings given them by section 551 of this title.

§ 702. Right of review

A person suffering legal wrong because of agency action, or adversely

SEC. 10(a).

affected or aggrieved by agency action within the meaning of a relevant statute, is entitled to judicial review thereof.

§ 703. Form and venue of proceeding

The form of proceeding for judicial review is the special statutory review proceeding relevant to the subject matter in a court specified by statute or, in the absence or inadequacy thereof, any applicable form of legal action, including actions for declaratory judgments or writs of prohibitory or mandatory injunction or habeas corpus, in a court of competent jurisdiction. Except to the extent that prior, adequate, and exclusive opportunity for judicial review is provided by law, agency action is subject to judicial review in civil or criminal proceedings for judicial enforcement.

SEC. 10(b).

§ 704. Actions reviewable

Agency action made reviewable by statute and final agency action for which there is no adequate remedy in a court are subject to judicial review. A preliminary, procedural, or intermediate agency action or ruling not directly reviewable is subject to review on the review of the final agency ac-

SEC. 10(c).

tion.   Except as otherwise expressly required by statute, agency action otherwise final is final for the purposes of this section whether or not there has been presented or determined an application for a declaratory order, for any form of reconsideration, or, unless the agency otherwise requires by rule and provides that the action meanwhile is inoperative, for an appeal to superior agency authority.

§ 705. Relief pending review

When an agency finds that justice so requires, it may postpone the effective date of action taken by it, pending judicial review.   On such conditions as may be required and to the extent necessary to prevent irreparable injury, the reviewing court, including the court to which a case may be taken on appeal from or on application for certiorari or other writ to a reviewing court, may issue all necessary and appropriate process to postpone the effective date of an agency action or to preserve status or rights pending conclusion of the review proceedings.

SEC. 10(d).

§ 706. Scope of review

To the extent necessary to decision and when presented, the reviewing court shall decide all relevant questions

SEC. 10(e).

of law, interpret constitutional and statutory provisions, and determine the meaning or applicability of the terms of an agency action. The reviewing court shall—

(1) compel agency action unlawfully withheld or unreasonably delayed; and

(2) hold unlawful and set aside agency action, findings, and conclusions found to be—

(A) arbitrary, capricious, an abuse of discretion, or otherwise not in accordance with law;

(B) contrary to constitutional right, power, privilege, or immunity;

(C) in excess of statutory jurisdiction, authority, or limitations, or short of statutory right;

(D) without observance of procedure required by law;

(E) unsupported by substantial evidence in a case subject to section 556 and 557 of this title or otherwise reviewed on the record of an agency hearing provided by statute; or

(F) unwarranted by the facts to the extent that the facts are subject to trial de novo by the reviewing court.

In making the foregoing determinations, the court shall review the whole record or those parts of it cited by a party, and due account shall be taken of the rule of prejudicial error.

* * *

§ 3105. Appointment of hearing examiners

Each agency shall appoint as many hearing examiners as are necessary for proceedings required to be conducted in accordance with sections 556 and 557 of this title. Hearing examiners shall be assigned to cases in rotation so far as practicable, and may not perform duties inconsistent with their duties and responsibilities as hearing examiners.

Sec. 11 (1st sentence).

§ 7521. Removal

A hearing examiner appointed under section 3105 of this title may be removed by the agency in which he is employed only for good cause established and determined by the Civil Service Commission on the record after opportunity for hearing.

Sec. 11 (2d sentence).

§ 5362. Hearing examiners

Hearing examiners appointed under section 3105 of this title are entitled

Sec. 11 (3d sentence).

to pay prescribed by the Civil Service
Commission independently of agency
recommendations or ratings and in accordance with subchapter III of this
chapter and chapter 51 of this title.

§ 3344. Details; hearing examiners

An agency as defined by section 551
of this title which occasionally or temporarily is insufficiently staffed with
hearing examiners appointed under
section 3105 of this title may use hearing examiners selected by the Civil
Service Commission from and with the
consent of other agencies.

SEC. 11 (4th
sentence).

§ 1305. Hearing examiners

For the purpose of sections 3105,
3344, 4301(2) (E), 5362, and 7521 and
the provisions of section 5335(a) (B)
of this title that relate to hearing examiners, the Civil Service Commission
may investigate, require reports by
agencies, issue reports, including an
annual report to Congress, prescribe
regulations, appoint advisory committees as necessary, recommend legislation, subpena witnesses and records,
and pay witness fees as established for
the courts of the United States.

SEC. 11 (5th
sentence).

*

INDEX

INDEX

INDEX
References are to Pages

APPROPRIATIONS
Administrative agency, 31–32

ASH COUNCIL
See Administrative Organization

ASHBACKER DOCTRINE
See Comparative Hearings

BANKING
Informal administrative process, 103–104
Primary jurisdiction, antitrust laws, 62
Summary procedure, 103–104
Supervision of, 103–104

BIAS
See, also, Combination of Functions
Generally 225–233

Administrative agency, private representation in, 229–230
Agency officer, removal for, 231
Combination of functions, and, 224–225, 233–236
Congressional influence, 227–228, 232
Examiner, removal for, 231
Judicial process, compared, 226
Judicial review, affected by, 230–231
NLRB, 226–227
Necessity, rule of, 230–231
Speeches, as reflected in, 228

CAB
Comparative hearings, 177
Rulemaking, statutory hearing and retroactivity, 149–151

CASE OR CONTROVERSY
See Constitution; Standing

CERTIORARI
See Judicial Review, Certiorari

CIVIL RIGHTS COMMISSION
Investigations by, 78

CROSS EXAMINATION—Continued

Adjudicative procedure, see Adjudicative Procedure, Cross examination

DECISION

See Initial Decision

DECLARATORY ORDERS

Generally, 118–119

DELEGATION

See, also, Constitutional Limitations; Judicial Review; Public Interest

Broad authority upheld, 20–21

Constitutional division of power, 6–11

Criminal penalty, 22

Due process, 22–24

Private representation, 230

Examiners, of trial authority to, 219

Invalid, 16–20

Investigation, power of, 77

Judicial power, of, 24

Judicial review, required, 22

Law-making powers, 7–9, 12–22

Legislative control, 30

Named contingency standard, 12–15

Narrowly construed, 20

Private groups, 23

Procedural protections, significance of, 16–19, 22–24

Public interest standard, 9–10

Separation of powers, 6–11, 25

Standards, theory of, 16, 26–27

Subdelegation, of agency trial authority, 219

Void for vagueness, 23–24

DISCLOSURE

See Publicity

DISCOVERY

See, also, Investigations

Adjudicative procedure, see Adjudicative Procedure

Administrative files, 40–41

INDEX
References are to Pages

INDEX
References are to Pages

INDEX

PUBLICATION
Code of Federal Regulations, 18
Federal Register, 18
Notice, of administrative hearings, 171–172
Rules,
    Final in Code of Federal Regulations, 127–128
    Final in Federal Register, 127–128
    Notice in Federal Register, 127

PUBLICITY
Administrative agency, affected by, 37–41
Administrative penalty, as a, 110–112
APA, § 3, § 552, 40–41
FDA, 110–111
HEW, cranberry scare, 110
Investigations, generally, 96–99
Judicial review, interrelationship of, 44–45
Limitations of, 41
Ombudsman, 39
Press releases, 110–111
Private groups, criticism of agencies, 37–38
SEC, 111
Tort remedies, 111–112

REQUIRED RECORDS
See Self Incrimination

RES JUDICATA
Adjudication, 64
    Rules developed in, 64–65
    Subsequent complaints in, 66–68
Estoppel, see Estoppel
FTC, 66–68
ICC, 65
Licenses, 65–66
Ratemaking, 64–65
Rulemaking, 64
Rules, general applicability, 64–65

RESIDUUM RULE
See Evidence, Residuum rule

INDEX

INDEX